THE DANCE WORKSHOP

ROBERT COHAN
—THE—
DANCE
WORKSHOP

Foreword by Wayne Sleep
Photography by Fausto Dorelli

London Contemporary Dance School

DANCE BOOKS
CECIL COURT LONDON

A GAIA ORIGINAL

Written by Robert Cohan

Performed by members of the London Contemporary Dance
Theatre (disbanded July 1994) and various jazz artistes

Photography by Fausto Dorelli

Direction:	Joss Pearson Lucy Lidell
Editorial:	Michele Staple
Design:	Sara Mathews Chris Meehan
Illustrations:	Peter Mennim with Sheilagh Nobel, Ann Savage and Joe Robinson
Paintings:	Barbara Karban

First published in 1986.
This edition published 1997.

Copyright © 1986 by Gaia Books Ltd., London

Dance Books Ltd
15 Cecil Court
London WC2N 3EZ

British Library Cataloguing in Publication Data
Cohan, Robert
The dance workshop.
1. Modern dance
I. Title   II. Dorelli, Fausto
793.3'2   GV1783

ISBN 1 85273 051 X

Printed and bound in Spain by
Artes Graficas Toledo S.A.

To the memory of Martha Graham with deep admiration and in appreciation

How to Use this Book

The exercises contained within this book provide a good foundation for any kind of dance training – contemporary, ballet or jazz. Use them as a back-up to your regular class, or if you are just beginning, as a guide to get you started in your own home.

There are three workout sessions in this book: Basic, Development and Jazz. Concentrate on the *Basic Workout* sessions first, and then, as you gain confidence, venture into the *Development Workout*, which contains more advanced exercises. Building on the basic exercises, the *Jazz Workout* provides a good introduction to jazz dance, and will enable you to vary your regular workout (which you must practise diligently!).

A word of warning about the exercises: don't just plunge into the first one, without reading the instructions on how to follow a sequence. These are given on page 54. The Workout Charts (pp.100-1, 148-9,184-5) will also help you to pace yourself by giving you a logical sequence of training.

A note, too, about the photographs used throughout this book. Rather than showing a student doing the exercise as it is taught on the page, these pictures portray a dancer's expressive performance of the movement, as part of a live dance sequence. The photographs are there to inspire, not teach; they will remind you that whatever exercise movements you learn, how you use and interpret them is what dance is all about.

CAUTION: It is important that you follow the exercises step-by-step, finding your own pace. Always warm up properly before working out, especially before jumps or leaps, and never strain in a position. If you ever experience a twisting or sticking pain in the joints during a session, stop at once. Remember, there is no need to rush or force yourself – all bodies are different, and it is up to you to find your own level. The exercises are safe for people of normal fitness, only if care and common sense are used.

Foreword
by Wayne Sleep

I first met Robert Cohan in the late 60s when he had come over from America to form the London Contemporary Dance Theatre Company, and I had just joined the Royal Ballet. This was the real beginning of contemporary dance in England, and of my own career as a classical dancer. The impact and style of Robert Cohan's new company of dancers greatly influenced me – in fact it was through their work that I first realised that classical dancing was not the only way. This book is bound to open the eyes of many more people, dancers and non-dancers alike.

The Dance Workshop demonstrates that dance is for everybody. Anyone who reads it, whether already training or a complete newcomer, should be able to enjoy the exercises – at any age from eight to eighty. Robert Cohan has put them together with great skill and careful attention to detail. He explains dance in a way which is readily understandable, and all his exercises are illustrated with absolute clarity, in a visual style which amply captures the sense of movement and the spirit of the dancers.

Dancing is a marvellous way of expressing yourself. It takes practice, of course – you must be careful not to overdo it at first, and build up slowly. But don't get discouraged – dance gives you a discipline for life, whether you take it up professionally or not. Most of all, it gives you joy.

I branched out from my classical roots to bring dance to a wider public as an *entertainment* and not just a high elitist artform.

DANCE IS FUN! It lifts the spirit, strengthens the body, and stimulates the mind, as I think this book clearly shows. Thank you, Robert Cohan.

Wayne Sleep

Contents

Introduction

Movement is as natural and as important to human life as breathing air. And just as all living bodies breathe, so, if you choose to define dance in its broadest sense, do all moving bodies dance.

Dance is a sign of life pressing itself out through the body, which is why it is so exciting to see and to do. It both stirs us with its energy, and satisfies us with its harmony. We all naturally want to move in harmony with the world – in harmony with other people, with the objects around us, and, in a more abstract sense, with our own lives. No-one likes the feeling of being clumsy – of bumping into chairs, or tripping on a paving stone. There seems to be an idea of grace that we all aspire to within ourselves.

Such feelings are at the essence of dance. Going to classes, and dancing itself, are ways of working on your life so that some part of it acquires grace and harmony, in a world that sometimes seems to have become too chaotic and too cluttered to live in. Much in the same way that some people make beautiful gardens to sit or wander in, dancers make gardens of movement inside themselves. These gardens, or ideas of how to move, are expressed as dances, and when we see them we understand some part of that dancer's life.

Dance speaks in a very special language, both to the doer, and to the watcher. It speaks of things "read between the lines", things that are impossible to put into words. Young people often find it especially satisfying to be involved in dance when they don't yet have the language to express the complicated emotions and ideas involved in growing up. Adults find dance brings to the surface emotions and feelings that often cannot be reached, or acknowledged.

The Benefits of Dance

Unless our natural responses are deadened by a restricted upbringing, we all would like to be able to dance in some way. We all move differently when happy or elated, and celebrate social events with music and dancing. The smallest children, even before they can walk properly, will bounce and sway to music.

Dance exercises the whole being. It helps you to feel at home in your body, to be aware of it, even to be friends with it again as you were in childhood. More than this, dance develops your inner discipline, your sensitivity to others, and your awareness of your own feelings – valuable strengths in your daily life. Best of all, as a way of taking exercise it is fun – involving a release of energy which allows you to dance just for the joy of living.

To start with, you will obviously gain physical strength from doing dance exercises on a regular basis. But it will be the kind of strength that will be in keeping with your own body proportion. You should not develop large thighs or big arm muscles from dance work, but rather strengthen your whole body the way it is. This doesn't mean that you won't change your physical shape – you certainly can change your shape radically through dance exercises, but you will have to do the workout every day (and, if you are overweight, diet in some way as well).

Even if you only work out three times a week, however, you should soon begin to notice an improvement in your physical stamina. Most of us lead much more sedentary lives than we should for our health.

The human body is designed and made to move. If you are forced to stay in one position for a long period of time, the need to move, to stretch, becomes overwhelming. It is the same need that we have for water, for food, for breath. A great part of the circulatory system of your body is achieved by muscular movement. The contraction of the muscles helps pump the blood back to the heart, as well as moving the lymph around our bodies. You will find that at the end of a dance workout, while you may be tired physically, you will at the same time feel much brighter and clearer. You will be able to think more lucidly, and should actually be calmer and more focused than you were before.

The type of workout that dance gives you is arguably better for most people than aerobics or jogging. It is now becoming well known that, for some people, jogging puts too much sudden stress on the heart, while aerobics, for all its good points, puts excessive wear and tear on some of the leg tendons and joints. Dance exercises, by contrast, build slowly throughout the class, so that you will not wear out one part of yourself first. And the kinds of movement that are involved in dance are those that build muscular stamina, while strengthening the heart and lungs slowly and carefully.

The dance workout will give you an opportunity to work on yourself in very specific ways. You will be concentrating on particular movements and muscular coordination. And when you finally accomplish them, the sense of achievement will give you enormous satisfaction.

As you stay with the training, the effects will show in your daily life. You will be more aware of yourself, walk with more grace and stand with more poise. And when you start to use and interpret the dance movements you have learned as a means of self-expression, there will be more dramatic changes – for you will become more aware of your feelings, and how to communicate them.

Students of the London Contemporary Dance School relaxing between classes.

Probably the most important change of all that regular dance training will bring about will be to put you in touch with yourself – with your body, your emotions, your powers of concentration, memory and logic. You will rediscover your body: analyse how it's working; figure out why it's not working well enough, and how you can change what may be bad physical habits or habitual ways of moving. You may want to strengthen and stretch yourself; to change the way your body feels to you; to make it more responsive and sensitive to your demands.

As you try to improve your body's movements, you will collide head-on with your emotions – which may have been in total control of your body until now. You are going to have to convince them that what you are doing will be helpful to all of yourself, and that the dancing body will ultimately be a better vehicle through which the emotions can express themselves.

You will also have to remember all that you are doing, all of the time, and why. A dance movement cannot be done with only part of your attention, because everything depends on *how* you do it. What you are doing is of only minor importance – there are many different ideas of which exercises to do, or what technique to learn. But everything comes together in the *"how"* – the quality with which you move. All good dancers have this quality; when we watch them we are always excited first by *how* they move, or *how* they do the steps. They may be the same steps you have seen many times before; but the way they are done makes them appear new and magical. This impact is achieved by attentive remembering, not by daydreaming.

Movement is logical; in fact, it has to do with the same kind of logic that physics uses. You will learn, from the inside, what the actions of levers, ball-and-socket joints and counterbalances feel like. You may not be able to write the equations, but you will be able to make and understand the movements. This being in touch with yourself for part of every day will have a focusing effect on you. It will make you more self-reliant, and may help you to feel more centred – not only physically, but mentally as well.

Dancing Nature
Nature is filled with activities that we can call dance. Even plants, as time-lapse photography shows, move in graceful, rhythmic and ordered ways. Of course they toss in the wind or droop in rain. But they also actively turn during the day to face the sun, and move to fertilize themselves or to disperse seeds. Some even move in long slow spirals for reasons not yet understood.

We have all seen the way male pigeons puff up their chests, spread their tails and dance around female pigeons – bobbing their heads up and down, ducking under, and running very quickly in little circles. It's a delightful and familiar dance routine, whose steps we know by heart. Swans, too, have a special dance – they glide in graceful tandem on the water, ducking their heads under and raising them together, finally entwining their necks like a lovers' knot. Manchurian cranes are perhaps the most enchanting of all dancing birds – pointing, stretching, leaping and bowing to each other in courtly, ritual display (*see right*). Many birds dance in groups, with perfect coordination. Flamingos run in huge flocks wheeling and turning, charging and stopping in the most carefully choreographed routines. Once while in Israel I saw thousands of small black birds form themselves into a huge spinning cone shape, just a few metres off the ground, and so travel slowly up a valley, like a living black cyclone. Not a single bird destroyed the perfect symmetry of this extraordinary dance.

All animals have dances – displays showing territorial possession, aggressive dances showing strength, excited solo performances to attract attention. Some, like otters, even have dances that are just high-spirited fun.

Humans have dances of the same kind, and many more, too. Anthropological studies show that people have used dance as an integral part of their culture since as far back in time as human groups can be traced. All over the world today, there are tribes and communities that have not changed their culture for thousands of years, and still use dance in their social lives. There are dances to welcome the sun, and dances for the night and the moon. There are dances where gods are enticed to take over the human performers' bodies, and so enter the community directly, and dances to appease the angry gods of volcanoes or earthquakes, or to end drought and bring rain.

Many of these dances survive in our own "civilized" social systems, little disguised. One of the most obvious and widely practised is the War Dance – though we call it a "parade". Courtship and preening dances like those of the pigeons take place every night in our discos, while the stylized and formal tribal dances used to bring God to earth are the predecessors of our religious ceremonies.

East and West

In the Far East, dance is still a part of the daily life for much of the population. It is used to tell stories and legends that are an important part of their cultural history, and also as a form of religious expression by special dancers or priests, and

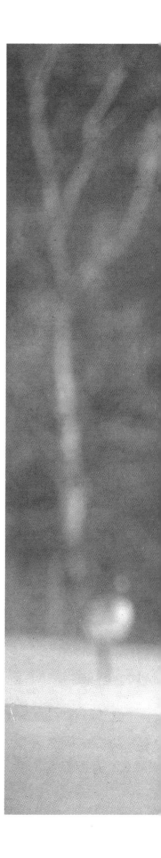

in some cases by the entire community. In Bali, for example, where dance is deeply rooted in the people's religious feelings, dancers will enact ritual dramas to ward off evil spirits, and the whole community will participate in the event (*see right*).

Dance communicates on many different levels at once, not relying as words must on a single language or type of education, and is therefore ideal as a means of expression in countries with many different dialects or even languages. And since Eastern dances are often allegorical, or tell a religious story designed to help people live life in a richer way, they are open to differing levels of interpretation both on the part of the performer and on the part of the audience. It is a marvellous experience to see one of these dances being performed in a village square, with everybody understanding the dance's meanings at his or her own level, from young children to grandparents.

In 1956 I was a dancer in the Martha Graham Company on a six-month tour of the Far East. In the United States at that time, Martha Graham's choreography was still considered *avant garde* and difficult to understand. But we performed her work in every Eastern country from Japan to Iran and were well received by all – except in Kuala Lumpur, where our audience consisted solely of British colonials! In many Eastern countries, dance is as well understood a means of expression as speaking, with the result that the villagers are adept at communicating those things that cannot be put into words. This is a form of expression we don't even consider important in our Western society, except in music – which speaks of quite different things than dance.

Dance in the West took a separate course from the East in its development. Records of dance during the Dark Ages are few, although folk dancing and ritual celebrations almost certainly continued. A social difference in the style of dance started to emerge in the Middle Ages, where in the courts the style reflected more refined social manners, while outdoors a more boisterous form of dance was enjoyed by the peasantry. It wasn't until the Renaissance, however, that dance emerged as an art form under the inventiveness of the 15th-century Italian dance masters, who served not only as instructors but as choreographers, creating dances around a basic dramatic or emotional idea. Steps were codified, and dancers were expected to be noble, dignified and responsive. The dances themselves were called "Ballets", and their steps were made up from a combination of entertainer acrobatics and a kind of traditional folk dance. This new Italian dance technique was later to influence the French kings and their courts, and help shape the French *ballet de cour*.

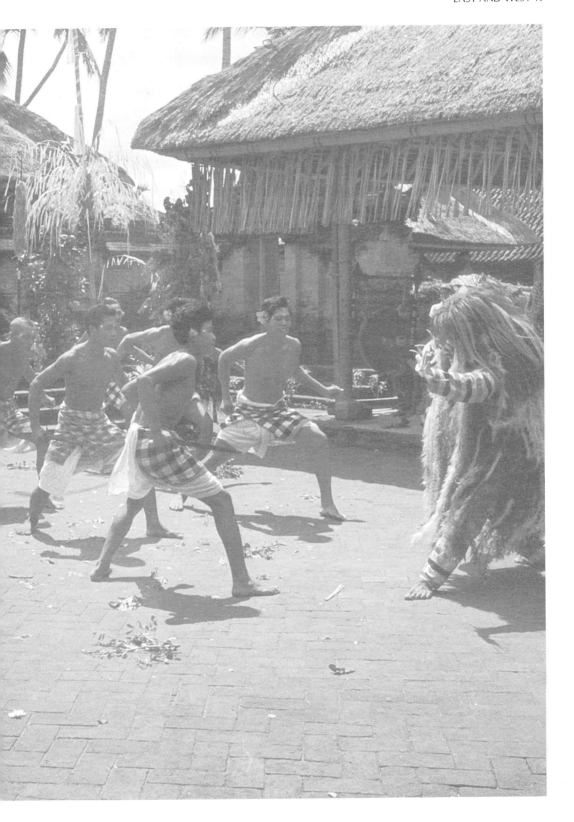

The Evolution of Dance

Every art form has its innovators, people who see the art in a new way, and are able to add a new point of view. Dance is no exception; the history of ballet is filled with the names of great artists who added their own personal ideas to enrich the art itself. Some were teachers who found a new way to teach; many were the dancers themselves who were able to perfect their bodies and techniques, to stretch their ability and to dance more complicated steps. Some dancers, like Marie Taglioni (1804-1884), had a natural physical advantage: she had very long arms, and by making a feature of them was able to add a new lyricism to the art of dance; another, Carlotta Grisi (1819-1899), was able to dance extremely fast, and so added very rapid footwork to the concept of what was possible.

Just as athletes of today are able to break records that a few years ago seemed impossible to reach, so dancers are able to learn from the previous generation and build new and better dance abilities. The same is true of the people who create the dances themselves: the choreographers.

Isadora Duncan (1878-1927) was one of those rare artists for whom the way things are – the established norm – is not good enough. Finding every aspect of dance at the turn of this century restrictive, she threw off the corsets of the Victorian era, together with the shoes and, most important of all, the ideas. Isadora changed the very idea of what you could dance *about*. And because she needed to say new and different things with her body, she had to discover a wholly new technique – fresh unfamiliar movements, different from any that had ever before been seen on a stage.

It is true to say that Western dance was never the same again. Her performances in Russia were so successful that she deeply influenced the ballet there, an influence which in turn was spread all over the world by the enormous success of the Diaghilev Company, when it came out of Russia to tour in the 1920s.

In the United States another innovative dance company, the Denishawn Company, was established in the early 1900s by Ruth St Denis and Ted Shawn. They, too, changed what you could dance about, and thrilled their audiences with a curious dance mixture consisting of ethnic forms (such as Indian or Spanish), ballet, their own original modern dance, and a great theatrical flair. Jazz at that time was also emerging as a popular dance form, and its effect on dance was not only to liberate the dancers, but also dance itself. Rules and restrictions were giving way to spontaneous vitality, and people were becoming more receptive to new ideas in dance. The Denishawn Company was especially

successful in training dance artists who saw dance as an art form to be personally explored, in the same way that painters such as Picasso, Matisse and Van Gogh were exploring and experimenting with art in Paris. These dancers became the next generation of choreographers in the United States; again, dance as an art form grew richer, more imaginative, surpassing its earlier limits.

Many Denishawn artists went on to teach their particular vision of dance, and to form their own companies. One of these was Martha Graham (1894-1991), with whom I worked for about 20 years. She had an unusually rich career: breaking away from Denishawn in 1923, she first performed her own dances in 1926, and, at 96 years of age, still created new and beautifully choreographed works. Martha Graham had a deep understanding of the source of movement, and the gift of teaching that elusive secret to her pupils. She, too, changed the ideas of what one can dance about, creating dances that tell of a woman's consuming jealousy (as Medea), of the despair of Jocasta discovering she has married her own son, Oedipus; dances that tell of the martyrdom of Saint Joan, or of the joy of a bride on her wedding day in the Appalachian Mountains. Each of these innovative ideas has ultimately enriched the vocabulary of dance itself.

Contemporary Dance

There is a clear distinction between the dramatic choreographed movement that is performed on the stage, and the technically oriented movement learned in the dance class; but they should be related. As the demands on dancers' ability become greater, so must the training adapt to reflect these new demands and prepare the dancers for the choreographers' ever-expanding vocabulary.

In modern dance, the technique itself prepares you for the demands of choreography. By teaching the sources of movement as a part of the technical training, modern dance makes you work deep within your own body, so that at times your instinctive responses can come into play and help you to learn to dance. There are very few inhibiting rules, aside from basic, logical ones about the placement of the body and the use of the legs and arms to keep you from injuring yourself. There are certainly no rules about style or body design; instead, you use your own sense of design to form yourself as a dancer in your own image.

When Robin Howard invited me to help him form the London Contemporary Dance Theatre in 1969, there was a very small audience for contemporary dance in Britain. But this was only because most people didn't know what it was. When they

did come, and experienced what dance can say and how deeply it can affect your emotions and feelings, they returned to performances again and again. Now there is a large, enthusiastic and loyal contemporary dance audience in Britain; they come to see dance because it gives them something special – something that can be gained in no other way.

Starting to Dance

If you are thinking of dance as a career, it does help to start early – eight to ten years old for simple basic training, through to 13 for more intensive work, and from 14 on for careful professional training.

But although starting early is generally best, it is not always so. You should start early only if good training is available – the single greatest reason that applicants for the London Contemporary Dance School were turned down was that they had received bad training while young, and I am sure this applies to other dance schools as well. It is also true that if you have a well formed athletic body and have trained in sports like swimming, running, jumping, or gymnastics, you may find you can start dance training in your late teens and still do very well, especially if you are male and taking up contemporary dance, rather than ballet.

I started dance training at the Martha Graham School in New York City when I was just 21. Patrick Harding-Irmer, who became a lead dancer with LCDT, did not start until he was 22. Of course, the later you start, the harder you must work in order to overcome the lost years of training. But you have some advantages too; older students tend to have more ability to concentrate and focus their resources, and consequently learn more quickly.

The major difficulty in starting late is being objective enough about your own physical potential. People who "discover" dance as adults and want to become dancers usually have all of the will power and passion necessary – but sadly, may simply not have the right bodies, nor the physical capacity to reach performance standard. Still, the magic touch of dance can be part of one's life in many other ways.

Not everyone wants to dance on a stage; dance is a very rewarding activity, for its own sake. I have taught many classes to non-professionals, and many times the same thing has been said to me. "These classes are the only time of the day that I really feel is *for me* – where I can work, for myself, on myself." This "personal space" that dance training gives is the very reason why dance is now so very popular, on an amateur level, in community centres and arts centres right across the country.

Dancers rehearsing at *The Place*, the home of the London Contemporary Dance Theatre.

Overleaf The author instructing a class at the London Contemporary Dance School.

The best way to learn to dance is under the care and direction of a good teacher. But you will only get out of a dance class what you bring to it – if you go to a dance class without much information about dance, it can all seem too bewildering and difficult to put together, no matter how good the teacher is. This book is designed to give you some understanding of what will be expected of you, and how to approach what you will learn. It will also serve as a constant companion during your training and practice. The exercises taught in this book are a good foundation for any kind of dance training – contemporary, ballet or jazz. They are not an end in themselves, but rather tools with which you can help your own dancing body to grow and emerge. Some suggestions of how the movements you are learning can build into a personal dance repertoire are given in the Dance Sequences (pp.102-5, 148-51).

It may be that you cannot find a teacher where you live, or that dance classes are inconvenient. Although it is difficult to work alone, if you go through the workout in this book, you should begin to understand and enjoy dance in a different and deeper way. It may be easier to keep going and follow the exercises if you can work with one or two friends. You could also use this workout in addition to attending dance classes – perhaps you can only manage to attend two classes a week, or even one, but you can still do two or three workouts at home each week between classes.

When you start dance training you should buy some dance clothes. The basic costume consists of tights and a leotard. All the rest of the currently popular dance fashion clothes are unnecessary. Leg warmers are used to help the legs warm up more quickly, but should be taken off once you are warm; the same is true of ankle warmers and sweat or training pants. Of course, the new dance clothes are fun and if they will give you more confidence or make you feel better, by all means buy them. If you are going to classes, though, do avoid bright colours until you find out if they are suitable – most serious teachers are put off by beginners wearing outrageous clothes. You should also take off all your jewellery, and tie your hair back if possible; you are in the studio to work and should come prepared accordingly. If there are many people in the class, be sure to put yourself in a place where you can see and hear the teacher. Be sensitive to where the other people in the class are standing or sitting, and try not to intrude on anyone else's space.

A good teacher will explain the material, present the exercises clearly and point out corrections. There are some teachers who just "give" a class: they present movements to you and don't say very much about how to do them. Even

if the movements are interesting, such classes are only useful if you know what you are doing. Don't hesitate to ask questions. Good teachers don't mind this, but do be sure you don't monopolize their time; they are trying to spread themselves out to all the students. Learn to use the mirror as an objective eye, to study your own body. In the studio try to be in a position where you can see yourself; at home do the standing work in front of a mirror. It will be a long time before you can simply "feel" what your body is doing; until then, you will constantly have to check in the mirror.

Before you begin, bear in mind that there is no hurry. You should approach the work in this book intelligently and not do it all at once. Dance takes years to do well; it is a cumulative process, and one goal will lead to another. Right from the beginning, though, you will enjoy it, and feel better. And once you have established it as a part of your weekly routine, you will find that dance enhances the quality of your life.

The Elements of Dance

When you start to learn dancing, it is important to recognize the elements or tools a dancer needs to acquire. In this chapter I have concentrated on the eight elements I consider to be the most vital for dance – Centering, Gravity, Balance, Posture, Gesture, Rhythm, Moving in Space and Breathing. You may not understand them all at first, but that doesn't matter. Simply read them through for now, then read them again periodically as you progress in the workshop – your understanding will change as you begin to discover what they mean in your own body.

The first element is one that is fundamental to your ability to dance well – Centering. It is centering or maintaining a sense of your own body centre that holds you together as you move. As your feeling of centering becomes clearer, you will enjoy the way it allows you to move freely and gracefully.

Gravity, the second element, is the force that holds you down on the earth. It is a force you must learn to work with because it constantly inhibits movement. One of the ways of working with it is by achieving Balance, our third element. Balance is concerned with more than the ability to balance on one leg. In dance, your aim is to achieve and constantly maintain an inner balance of the whole body. It is this kind of balance we mean when we talk of a room in which the furniture is nicely arranged as well-balanced. It is a tension of mutual support among all the parts that brings the whole together in a new way.

Posture, or body alignment, is closely linked with Centering, Gravity and Balance, and will improve automatically as you develop the first three elements, though you will also have to work on it independently. To attain a good posture for dance you need to be able to change your perception of your body, for there is often a wide discrepancy between what feels and what looks right.

Gesture involves using your body as an expressive instrument to communicate feelings and ideas in patterns of movement. Anger, for example, is expressed in movement patterns very different from those elicited by joy or sadness. Rhythm, to my mind, is something that everybody has, though some people are not aware of or sensitive to it. We live our lives according to a complex interplay of cycles and rhythms – our hearts beat to one rhythm, our lungs breathe to another, our limbs move to yet another. Finding your sense of rhythm is largely a matter of paying attention.

The seventh element I call Moving in Space. When you dance, you need to be as aware of the space around you as a cat. A cat is never indifferent to the space it is moving through. Even when it comes to jumping up on to a sofa arm that it has leapt on to a thousand times before, it still moves with care and awareness, gauging the space with a calculating eye.

Our final element of dance is Breathing. At the beginning it is hard to coordinate breath and movement when you dance. But breathing well is crucial to dance, not only to bring more oxygen to the body but also to give your movement fluency and harmony.

When we look at a beautifully made piece of porcelain, say, or jewellery, we know how much thought and care has gone into creating such quality. It is this same kind of quality that we want to show in our bodies and this that is meant by technique – the sum total of all these tools of dance.

Centering

If all the work you did on yourself in dance had to be
expressed in one word it would have to be centering – your
ability to move, to hold, to organize yourself around your
own physical body centre. Just as the world orients its entire
mass around one measurable central point, maybe one atom,
so we have one identifiable central point in our bodies from
which we move. This is our physical centre. If you are
centred, you can eventually learn to do anything. If you are
not centred, you may develop beautiful-looking arms and
legs, but you will never be able to move well.

You can liken your sense of centre to your sense of place
or home. If you didn't have a strong sense of home, you
would probably get lost every time you went out. You know
your home. You remember it. You know directions from it,
like lines radiating out from a central point. No matter how
far you may travel, your recognition and remembrance of
home give you a basis for relating to the rest of the world.
Yet even though we are territorial animals, we still don't
know the territory within our own bodies.

If you were to balance your body like a see-saw across a
support, the point of balance would be close to your physical
centre. In most people, the body centre is one or two inches
below the navel, in the middle of the pelvis, depending on
the length and weight of the legs. This will all seem a bit
theoretical until you begin to feel your own centre.

Start by feeling how your arms and legs work from the
same central point in the back. Press one hand across the
muscles of your lower back, just below the waist. Now swing
your other arm and feel the muscles in your back moving.
Reduce the swing of your arm so that it is only one or two
inches and you will still feel your back muscles moving. The
same thing will be true of your legs. Now, still with one hand
pressing the lower back, walk around in a small circle,
swinging the free arm, and feel with your hand the
complicated muscle dance that is going on in the centre of
your lower back. Then stand still and see if you can lift your
free arm from that same point in your back. You will
immediately feel that you are moving with a deep physical
commitment, with understanding.

Once you begin to have a sense of moving from your
centre it will become easier to control movement. Think of
yourself on a moving carousel: if you ran around the edge,
you would have to run very fast just to keep up, but if you
were at the centre you could walk around its central pole
slowly and with control.

Gravity

Gravity is the force that pulls us down toward the centre of the earth. Its downward pull is so great that it is hard for us to jump up higher than a foot in the air. In fact, it is a wonder that we can stand on two legs at all!

The human body is a miracle of engineering. We tend to forget that it took years for our muscle groups and tendons to learn how to pull the bones straight up and balance the heavy head on the entire delicate structure. First we had to learn how to roll over, then to sit up, then to crawl, to stand shakily and finally to move, to walk and then to run. But as adults, the special skills acquired in infancy have been taken over by our autonomic movement centres, and now we move without thinking about it at all.

If you want to become a dancer, however, it is vital to become conscious again of the pull of gravity and to learn how to combat its force. Gravity is the constant you must always be aware of; understanding how to use and oppose its energy, its magnetic pull, is a skill that is basic to dance.

Try to become aware of the pulls in your own body. As you read this, what points in your body are taking the most weight? When you push down on those points can you feel how to rise up from them and perhaps hold yourself better? Look at the way people around you are standing. Observe the series of counterbalances necessary to stay in any one position. Think of the toll that gravity takes on older people, where the muscles are no longer strong enough to resist the downward pull. Then try imitating their postures to get a deep physical sense of the pull of gravity.

The more familiar you become with gravity's unrelenting energy, the more you will be able to free yourself from its pull. Do this three-part exercise to develop a sense of using and opposing gravity. Go up a staircase slowly, one step at a time, feeling incredibly heavy. Sense that each leg in turn is carrying your entire weight. Lean forward and put pressure on one leg at a time, allowing your body to relax downward. This will give you a feeling of gravity. Now go upstairs with your back straight and your back and leg muscles tight and lift your torso up as you push down on each leg in turn. Now you are using your muscles to overcome gravity. Finally, using your muscles as before, go upstairs again, but this time feel as if someone is pushing you up under the working buttock and the base of your spine is directing its energy up through your breastbone to the top of the stairs. In this way you are using your muscles and your will to overcome the gravity pull.

Balance

In dance, balance is not only a matter of balancing on one leg. It is, more importantly, the art of achieving an inner relationship between all the points of your body which you can hold in your awareness. It is not something you do once in a while – you should always be working on and developing your sense of balance whether you are moving or standing still. The problem lies in splitting your attention enough to be able to concentrate both on your inner balance and on the dance or movement you are making. With practice, you can do this quite easily by using imagery.

Hold one arm out in front of you and then imagine that it's floating on the surface of the sea. Let it respond to the movement of the watery surface; let it rise and fall easily as small waves run up its length. You will find a recognizable sensation of inner balance taking place in your muscles.

Now lift the other arm and imitate the sensation of balance you just discovered. This time, forget about the water and waves and try to be aware of the inner relationship of muscles, bones, joints, veins and nerves. If you can feel the sensation clearly, you could try to experience it over the entire body. As you read, put your body into a complicated position. Cross your legs, let yourself lean to one side, and counterbalance with your head. Now try to feel the inner relationship between parts of your body. Where is there pressure and weight? Is your spine curved, tilted, or stretched one way? Where are you counterbalancing the weight of your head? How far is your right foot from your left elbow? Can you memorize the position and take it up again later? Is it in balance? If not, change it slightly until you feel an inner harmony. Can you sense your entire body at once? A position that has internal balance may not necessarily look pretty or symmetrical but it will be aware.

The other aspect of balance is the actual art of balancing on both legs, or on one leg as so often happens in dance. If you can find inner balance, you are nearly there. To balance on one leg all you need do is to add the opposing muscular energies necessary to hold the position. In dance you will seldom take up positions that are symmetrically counterbalanced, like a see-saw. Most often the positions will be asymmetrical, needing complicated inner stress. But if you are aware internally of the need for and sensation of balance, you should be able to work them out.

Remember, balancing is an active state, a process that is constantly happening. If you forget to do it, you fall down.

Posture

Dancers work all their dancing lives on their body alignment, or posture. It is the key to balance and therefore to movement. Your posture not only reveals your feelings, but can actually produce feelings in you. For example, if you stand with knees slightly bent, pelvis slumped under, belly out in front, upper back rounded, neck short and head dropped forward, you will begin to feel terrible and unable to move well. See for yourself by doing it and then try to walk. Running is out of the question, as well as dancing – the feeling is all wrong, with the weight held low in the body. What can you do to correct these common postural faults?

Let's begin by learning how to stand properly. Start with the feet. Lift up your arches and let your weight fall on three points: the ball of the foot, the heel and the outside ridge. Make sure the ankle bones are straight and the sides of the heel are at right angles to the floor. Stretch the legs as long as you can so that the thighs are pulled up and the pelvis is sitting on the top of the thigh bones. Try to increase the space between the bottom rib and the top of the pelvic bone – the stomach will be drawn flat and the entire spine should feel long and stretched, with the neck fully extended. Relax your shoulders and let them hang from the spine. Carry the top of your head as high as possible. In this physical attitude you will actually begin to feel brighter and more aware.

The way you sit is just as important, especially for the floorwork exercises (see pp.56-69, 108-127). Try this experiment using a hard chair. First, sit down at the front of the chair and roll backward on your pelvis until your torso is slumped on the back of the chair. This is about the worst way you could possibly sit. Then do just the opposite. Sit straight up on the two sitting bones that form the bottom of your pelvis, imagining the pelvis to be a large bowl out of which the rest of the torso grows. Lengthen your spine and pull the abdomen flat by stretching up on the inside of your spine. Hold your neck up high and let the head float above it.

Now, keeping your spine stretched up, drop your shoulders down toward your hips and, at the same time, lift your arms up over your head. With your arms held up, raise your shoulders for a moment then drop them down again a few times to see how loose they are. Although it is hard to keep your shoulders down while lifting your arms, doing this exercise will make you see just how awkward it feels to raise them. And whilst you will find it hard to move in this position, in time your "old" posture will seem even more inhibiting.

Gesture

As a species, the human animal discovered far back in the distant past that its chances of survival were better in a social group than alone. It did not develop specialized claws, sharp teeth or a hard shell-like covering for protection, but instead had to rely for defence on a conceptual brain and the ability to communicate complex ideas to other members of the group. Ever since that time, we have been evolving ways of moving that show other humans what we are thinking. With subtle gestures and postural attitudes we show cooperation, give confidence to friends or display our aggression to enemies. Of course we can talk to one another, but even today a multitude of languages are spoken and the evidence is that it was little different in the past. So for us to communicate it was necessary to evolve a common language of gesture.

Dance companies from all over the world perform all over the world and with very few exceptions are understood everywhere they go. The exceptions exist where dance has become very formalized and attached to a religion, as in some Japanese dance, or where it is mime-like as well as religious, as with certain Indian dance schools, where the mime is a learned language. Even in these cases we can understand a great deal – but we understand far more where the dance movements are related to common gestures.

Arms crossed over the chest are a protective wall. Hands on hips mean "show me"; while fists on hips are even more challenging, demanding "prove it to me". Hands held out in front suggest you are ready to give or receive. Shaking right hands probably originated as a way of proving that you were not carrying a weapon when you met someone else.

Holding the head forward looks eager, cocking it to one side looks interested. Concern or sympathy are expressed by a hand held to your face, thought by curling the hand into a fist. Raising the shoulders is a gesture of not knowing or caring; holding the shoulders forward expresses pain. If you stand on one leg, with all your weight on one hip, you look as if you're waiting – tapping your foot in that position signifies impatience or boredom.

Observe yourself and those around you and learn to recognize what the body is saying. For almost every movement we make demonstrates a thought, a feeling or an attitude. These are the tools of dance and as such can be used to create sequences of movement that are stories of human experience.

Rhythm

A good sense of rhythm is essential for a dancer, but it can be a little complicated to acquire. We tend to think of people as being born with a sense of rhythm, but I think rhythm is always learned. Tribal people are believed to possess a natural affinity for rhythm. But if you observe tribal gatherings you will find that all the children are there, learning either drumming or dancing.

Rhythm is often learnt very early in life. Childhood exposure to music, and an encouraged response to rhythm and dancing while young, can certainly help later on. If you had no exposure to rhythm as a child, however, don't worry – all is not lost. Acquiring a sense of rhythm is more a matter of paying attention than anything else. Listen to any piece of popular music – one with a Latin rhythm is the easiest to use. See if you can find the most obvious beat – generally the beat is carried by the drums. Once you've got it, try to discern the "heavy" beats – the ones that stand out more than the others. Count how many lighter beats there are between each heavy beat, then try clapping the rhythm.

Now see if you can count the full rhythm – *1, 2, 3, 4, 2, 2, 3, 4,* or whatever the count is. When you can hear the beat quite clearly, try moving to it. Move on every beat, simply shifting your weight from one hip to the other, keeping your feet still. Try to hear only the beat, not the rest of the music. Once you can move exactly on every beat, not before or after, try moving on the first three beats, say, and holding still on the fourth. (Adapt your movement accordingly if the music has less or more than four beats.) Next move only on beats one and two and hold still for three and four. Then try moving only on beat one or four; and finally move on whichever beat you like, without losing the rhythm.

When working on your sense of rhythm, it is important to make sure that you are right on the beat, not slightly late. All the work that goes into making a beat has already been completed by the time you hear it. The drum has been hit, and the sound has travelled through space and vibrated your eardrum, registering in your brain as a beat. So to stay in rhythm, all your internal work must be done and your movement completed to time with the beat. In fact, to get it right, you have to anticipate the beat slightly. Feel as if you are making the beat with your body as well as hearing it. Try to be at one with it, rather than dancing to it.

Once you come to learn dance sequences, you will find that it is the rhythm and beat of the dance that form the "threads" which allow you to memorize the structure of the dance (see also Tempo, p.55).

Moving in Space

Our bodies were made to move. Over hundreds of thousands of years they have evolved to perform all the movements necessary for survival on the surface of this earth – to run on uneven ground, to walk long distances, to climb trees, to reach up, to dig down, to curl up and hide, to gather big fruits or tiny seeds. Our feet, legs and spine are incredibly complex and can adjust to the slightest variations of balance as we move. The same is true of our upper backs and arms. As well as being strong, they are able to perform very delicate tasks.

Our bodies evolved to move in the space around them, both near and far. Space is not just empty air but a tangible element to move through, just as water is a tangible element to a fish, determining its pattern of movement. Your arms, legs, neck and head are extensions of your body out into space, that make it possible for you to function. Look at an object near you that you can just reach if you extend your arm to it. Consider the space between you and the object as an area that you must go through. Imagine your hand and arm going through that space. Now very slowly let your hand start to move across the distance from yourself to that object. Consciously go through space.

Now choose something much further away that you will need to walk to in order to touch. See the distance as enormous. Feel what you will need to do in your body to move there – first shifting your entire body on to your legs, then moving your legs under you, keeping your balance, avoiding other objects, stopping just in time, and then finally reaching even further into space to touch the object. Now slowly do it. Feel your accomplishment as a journey through outer space.

The body may have evolved for very functional reasons necessary for its survival, but we can use its beautifully made form for other reasons: to express our thoughts and emotions, to actually press our feelings out of our torso and limbs in such a way as to show other people how we are feeling, and to satisfy our desire for movement. In fact, the desire to dance could be just an extension of that desire. Our muscles feel better when they are used, and once we get used to moving them, the whole body will respond by working in harmony with itself: to run, to turn, to leap, to dance.

Breathing

Every living creature breathes. But in dance it is not only the physical function of breathing that is important, it is also its use as an expressive tool, as part of the language of movement that conveys meaning. Fast, shallow breathing, for example, implies excitement or stress, while calm slow breathing suggests a certain degree of self-control.

More abstractly, the word breath is used in dance to denote a specific quality of movement. A dancer who has a "sense of breath" moves with freedom and harmony. A phrase of movement "with breath" has a controlled and considered extension in time, a clear beginning and end, no matter how fast or slow it is; a phrase "without breath" looks stiff or mechanical with no breathing space.

Breathing in harmony with your steps will give your movement a sense of calmness and fluency. But at first you will find it hard to breathe well while you dance. There are two main problems: how to exercise some control over your breathing without interfering with it; and how to use the ribcage properly, while still holding a high posture in the torso. These simple exercises will help you to become aware of the problems. Take a walk at a fairly quick tempo and see how many steps you are taking to each breath. Is it the same number when you breathe in as when you breathe out? Now change the timing of the breath. If you were breathing in every three or four steps, say, and out every three or four, raise the count to five or six. You can also vary the rate between in- and out-breaths. Breathe in for two steps and out for four. What does it feel like to split your concentration between walking and breathing? It is important to learn how to concentrate on two or three things at the same time, as you will frequently have to divide your attention while dancing.

You must also learn to breathe more deeply by expanding your ribs at the back of the body rather than the front. Fold your arms behind you, hands holding opposite elbows, and take a deep breath, trying to expand the back sideways to press the arms apart. Alternatively lean over from the hips with a straight back, taking your weight on your hands on a chair seat, and breathe in by expanding your back. If you are doing it right you will feel movement in the lowest ribs, as well as across the shoulders. The top of your chest should also move. Cross your arms over your chest, palms resting high on each side. Now as you take a deep breath, try to feel the lower ribs expanding right out of the back of the spine, then the whole back expanding, and finally the top of the chest lifting up under your hands. You should not feel the lower ribs expanding at the front, pushing your elbows out in front.

The Basic Workout

Training your body is exactly like training a new puppy. A relationship has to be established that will allow learning to take place. You have to be kind and firm both at the same time – intelligent or calculating in your demands on yourself and instinctive or intuitive in your response. Just like a young dog, your body will try to distract you from the training, and in many of the same ways. It will start to complain, to hurt and to collapse on you and you will have to coax it and convince it that it can do more. Your body will also get very excited – in fact at times it will run away from you. Used properly, this is a good energy that will allow you to accomplish a great deal in a short time, but if you don't learn to channel it, it will spill over and exhaust you.

It may seem as if I am overplaying the analogy between training an animal and training your body, but having trained both I know I am not. The idea implies the need for a certain objectivity toward yourself, whether you are teaching yourself to dance or learning from a teacher. By objectivity I don't mean self-criticism, although that may come into it, but the detachment to know whether or not you are moving on the beat, for instance, or to know whether or not your knee is straight.

Dancers work in front of mirrors just to establish this kind of objectivity, using the mirror as a cool dispassionate eye. Feelings cannot be trusted in dance, especially at the beginning. People with a bad posture stand that way because it feels all right to them. Before they can change their posture, their feeling or sense of themselves has to be changed from the subjective to the objective. Again and again, while working out the

material in this book, you will come up against this problem of changing your ideas of how your body is. It may sound daunting but it will be well worth it in the end as you discover a new world of experience and enjoyment right inside your own body.

While learning and practising the material in the Basic Workout, you should always set yourself a specific timespan to work, such as 45 minutes or an hour. There are sure to be times when you want to stop before that, but you should discipline yourself to stick to the time you set. In fact, you will find that you often work better after you've gained your second wind and passed through the obstacle of wanting to stop.

You should choose a time and a place to work where you won't be disturbed by noise or interrupted by other people. Unplug the telephone or cover it with a pillow. Working on yourself requires a particular kind of concentration and you won't be able to achieve this if there is any form of distraction. Clear a space for yourself that is large enough for you to work in before you start. The most important factor is continuity. Several 45-minute sessions a week on a regular basis are far more helpful than long intense sessions once in a while.

Like starting anything new, it is not going to be easy at first. But the rewards of learning to move well are enormous. You are going to feel brighter and more alive. You will succeed in achieving the specific movement goals that you set yourself and enjoy the inner satisfaction this brings. With hard work you will also actually change your physical shape. But more than this you will change the whole way you look and move as you create a new harmonious dancing body.

Sequence of Workout

The Basic and Development Workouts are broken down into three main sections – work done sitting or lying on the floor, known as Floorwork; work done standing up, but more or less on the spot, known as Centrework, and work that involves travelling across the floor or Moving in Space.

The **Floorwork** begins with simple exercises that are designed to concentrate attention on your body, especially on the torso. Then you will progress on to leg and arm exercises that develop coordination between your right and left sides. In **Centrework** you will be discovering a sense of your own centre. You will also be developing strength in the legs and combining it with the enormous power available to you when the back and legs work together. You will work first with the legs parallel, then turned out, which is necessary for developing speed and articulation of steps.

As you move and shift your weight around your centre, you will want to extend your movements in readiness for **Moving in Space**. Here you will learn to walk correctly, then practise variations on the basic walk that will enable you to move more easily and in different rhythms. Both workouts end with quicker movements, notably skips and leaps.

Learning the Exercises

If you are new to dance, don't start by rushing through every exercise. It will be much better for you to learn to do a few of them well, than to try to do too many, without understanding.

First, select your exercise (see the Basic Workout Chart, pp.100-1) and read through the introductory text. Some exercises may have more than one sequence using the same positions, therefore you must refer to the instructions headed "The Sequence" or "Sequence 1 (2, 3)" for the order in which you proceed and the tempo (see right). At the end of the instructions is the *sequence line*, which summarizes the exercise. It may look like this:

SP. A B C B D B x 4 (right side) **SP. A B C B D B** x 4 (left side)

In your mind, run through the positions in the order indicated, starting at SP (the starting position). The point after the SP means that you do not repeat the SP each time, and that SP is not included in the first count. If the exercise was on six counts, the first would be on A and the sixth would be on the third B. The "x 4 (right side)" indicates how many times you do the exercise on the right side. The same rules apply to the rest of the line, which repeats the exercise four times on the other side.

Now you are ready to try the positions. Read the captions carefully, imagining how any inner sensations mentioned may feel. Then do the sequence using the correct count and tempo. Don't stop if you make a mistake – try to complete the sequence. If necessary, do it at a very slow tempo until it is firmly implanted on your body's muscular memory. Only at this stage will you be able to devote most of your attention to observing yourself, and correcting your body's sensations.

1 **Introductory text** Introduces you to the exercise: what particular parts of your body you will be working on; different applications of the exercise; important sensations to look out for.

2 **Sequence instructions** The key to the exercise: indicates the order in which you follow the captions, the number of times you repeat the sequence, and the tempo (see above right).

3 **Sequence line** An annotated summary of the exercise (see left for explanation).

Tempo

All exercises in dance are performed at a fixed tempo or pace,
as indicated at the end of each
sequence text, before the
sequence line. The tempo provides
dancers with a way of knowing
where they should be in a
particular sequence at any given
moment. For the sake of simplicity,
I have used just four basic tempos
– fast, medium, slow or very slow.
I shall call a one-second beat a
medium tempo, a two-second
beat (i.e. one beat every two
seconds) a slow tempo and a
three-second beat very slow. A
fast tempo will be two beats per
second. Since most people have
quartz watches (or access to one),
you should be able to count one-
second beats quite accurately.
Practise with a watch until you
succeed in staying fairly close to
the recommended tempo without
looking.

Counting Dancers use a particular
method of keeping time, where
they change the first beat (the
"one") of each set of counts as a
way of recording how many sets of
counts they have done. For
instance, if you are instructed to
complete a sequence in four sets
of three counts, you would count
them as follows: *1,2,3; 2,2,3; 3,2,3;
4,2,3.* The counts, of course, would
be done at the chosen tempo.

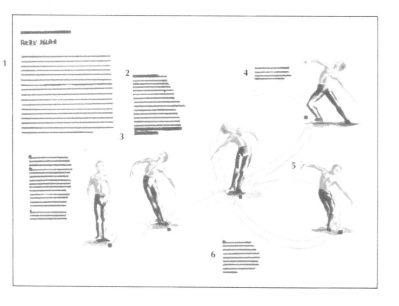

4 **Caption** Relates specifically to
the position illustrated; how
you should hold your body,
and what sensations you
should be feeling. Do *not*
proceed on to the next
caption without checking the
sequence order.

5 **Arrows** The pale orange
arrows help you to follow an
exercise through, as a
supplement – not a
replacement for – the
sequence line. They do not
indicate movement through
space – in this example, all
the movement occurs in one
place. Smaller blue arrows
(not shown here) near the
figure indicate direction of
stretch or movement.

6 **Transition steps** Sometimes
you will notice a position is
labelled T, T1 or T2. These are
transitional movements, often
done in between counts on
your way to the next position.

FLOORWORK

In Western society we have removed ourselves from the floor by the use of the chair. We consider ourselves more civilized for having done so, yet by doing this, we cause large muscle groups in our legs and backs to atrophy and many of our joints to stiffen with age. A 60-year-old Japanese woman who spends much of her day going from kneeling to standing will usually be far stronger and more flexible than a Western woman of similar age and status.

The following exercises are performed on the floor, either sitting, lying or kneeling. The main advantage of working this way is that you will be able to isolate muscle groups of the pelvis, legs and back, and work on them directly. You will also be able to stretch with minimal weight on the working tendons. You must remember, however, that you are on the floor to work, not to rest. Use it not merely to sit on, but also to push down against. In any floor position you should hold your body in such a way that if you were suddenly lifted up you would come away in one piece like a statue, and not with your legs dangling.

Sitting Spine Stretches

Your spine is a remarkable structure, made up of 24 bones or vertebrae from pelvis to neck. Each of these vertebrae is separated by a cushion of fluid-filled cartilage which acts as a shock absorber. It is these cushions of cartilage that give the spine its enormous flexibility and allow you to bend freely and with ease. Unfortunately, the potential for movement of the spine tends to be much underused, partly because we are not aware of it, but mainly because we allow the ligaments and muscles to tighten through lack of use.

When doing these spine stretches, think of the movement as flowing out of the spine and into the limbs. For this you need not only to make the spine flexible, but also to be fully aware and in touch with it. Try to experience the entire body from the inside – from the soles of your feet to the palms of your hands and the crown of your head. Your whole body should participate in the feeling of stretching the spine.

SP1

Sequence 1 On a count of two eights go from SP1 to A, exhaling as you curve over. On a further eight counts inhale and return to SP1. Repeat. Tempo: medium.

SP1. A SP1 x 2

SP1 Sit on the floor with knees bent, soles of the feet together, hands resting on the ankles, back straight, neck long and head held high.

A

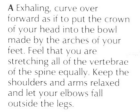

A Exhaling, curve over forward as if to put the crown of your head into the bowl made by the arches of your feet. Feel that you are stretching all of the vertebrae of the spine equally. Keep the shoulders and arms relaxed and let your elbows fall outside the legs.

Sequence 2 Start in the transitional position, T, and move into SP2 by opening your legs and arms out to the sides. Then in two counts of eight, exhale and curve over to position B. Inhale and return to SP2 on the third eight. Repeat the movement between SP2 and B once more before bringing your legs back together for the start of Sequence 3. Tempo: medium.

T SP2. B SP2 x 2

T (transition) Extend the arms and legs straight forward, feet stretched and pointed, heels off the floor.

SP2 Open the arms and legs out to the sides as far as they will comfortably go.

B Exhaling, stretch your body forward, so that the crown of your head is almost touching the floor. Make sure that your knees stay straight and facing upward, and that your feet are stretched. Rest your hands lightly on your shins.

Sequence 3 This exercise is also performed in three counts of eight, taking two eights to go over to C (exhaling), and one to return to SP3 (inhaling). After the second two eights, come up inhaling and cross your legs into position D. (This position will lead you into Breathing, *facing page*.) Tempo: medium.

SP3. C SP3 x 2 . **D**

SP3 Sit with arms and legs outstretched in front of you, as in T for Sequence 2, but this time flex your feet.

D Inhaling, stretch your feet and bring your legs back crossed in front of you. Rest your arms to the side, hands just touching the floor.

C Exhaling, repeat the same curving over of the spine, but keep your arms stretched forward beyond your feet. Try to touch your knees with the top of your head.

Breathing

Breathing is one of the few *movements* we make all the time, yet pay little attention to. Most of us breathe too shallowly, making little use of the diaphragm, so that only a small amount of oxygen is taken in. Breathing correctly involves the expansion and contraction of the entire chest, upper back and upper abdomen. To inhale, the lungs expand fully as the diaphragm moves down into the upper abdomen. To exhale, the abdomen contracts and the diaphragm moves up into the rib cage as air is expelled. These exercises show you how body movement affects the breath and vice versa, so that eventually your body and breath work in harmony. If you become dizzy, just lie down and breathe normally. You will simply have received more oxygen than you are used to.

Sequence 1 Using your breath to motivate the movement, exhale (SP), and then start to breathe in slowly, resisting the urge to straighten until the breath forces you to do so. At the top of the lift (A), hold your breath. Then carefully start to exhale back to SP. Take two counts to inhale, and two to exhale. Repeat three times. Tempo: very slow.

SP. A SP x 4

Sequence 2 Now, also in four counts, use the body to motivate the movement. Proceed from SP to A, but resist breathing in as you straighten your spine. You will find that the breath rushes into the lungs as the stretching sensation rises up the back and the rib cage expands. Hold your breath for a few moments, then return to SP by tilting the pelvis under and curving the lower back out, so that air is forced out of your body. Repeat three times. Tempo: very slow.

SP. A SP x 4

SP With your legs crossed and arms to the sides just touching the floor, sit up on the two bones that form the base of the pelvis. Exhaling, tuck your pelvis under, rolling to the back of these bones, and allow the spine to curve out to the back.

SP

A

B

A Breathe in, straightening first the pelvis, then the spine, working up toward the head, until you are sitting in an upright position, your torso lifted and fully expanded.

B Continue breathing in, lifting your chest even higher. Stretch your spine to arch the upper back, so that your face is turned to the ceiling.

Sequence 3 Start again in the exhaled position, SP, breathe in (A), but continue inhaling through to B. Take four counts to go from SP to B, and four more to return to SP. Repeat three times.

SP. A B A SP x 4

Contractions

It is strange that this movement to curve the spine, the contraction, should not have been included in dance training until the 1920s, with the advent of contemporary and jazz techniques. Strange because it is a very human movement that has always been used in all kinds of dance. As a dramatic gesture, not only can it be extremely expressive of pain and sorrow, but also of joy and laughter.

We shall see later (pp. 78, 86) how the contraction movement through space can be strong and forceful, activating the whole body, but here we are concerned simply with the sitting position on the floor.

SP

The Sequence In this exercise, you go from the release or straight-back position (SP) to the contraction (A) in three counts, returning in three counts to SP again. It is important to remember whilst doing this exercise that the contraction is a strong, stretching movement of the spine, not a shortening or collapsing one. Try to keep the height from the top of the head to the floor the same throughout. Repeat three times. Tempo: slow.

SP. A SP x 4

SP Sit with your legs crossed and your arms extended straight in front of you at shoulder level, hands clasped. Hold your back long and stretched up, and sit firmly on your two pelvic bones.

A Tighten your buttock muscles and tilt your pelvis under, starting a chain reaction up your back (as in Breathing, p.59), but this time feel your spine lengthening as you curve it outwards between the shoulder blades. Imagine that your pelvis is pushing into and servicing the muscles of the thighs, rather than retreating away from them. In an opposing movement, push your arms straight forward.

A

Leg Exercises

Many exercises that isolate specific leg muscles and develop leg coordination can be done on the floor. The advantage is that you don't have to worry about balance and shifting of weight. But you must use your legs with a great deal of muscular energy from the large buttock muscles. As you work, keep the spine stretched, the shoulder blades pressed down and the abdomen tight and up. It will help if you imagine that your body is travelling forward into your legs.

As you build up a rhythm, start to work the feet more deeply by resisting the energy to point them. You can do this by trying to hold the flexed-back position with the front part of the feet and toes. This will make you work the feet sequentially from the ankles down to the toes. The sensation is like massaging the feet with your own muscles.

The Sequence This exercise is on six counts: tighten 1 (A) , turn out 2 (B), stretch the feet 3 (C), flex the feet 4 (B), return to parallel 5 (A), relax 6 (SP). Repeat three times, then rest and repeat the sequence again. Tempo: slow.

SP. A B C B A SP x 4

After some experience you can cut the first and sixth counts out by doing the entire exercise without relaxing the muscles (effectively making A into the SP). The exercise will be on four counts.

A. B C B A x 4

SP Sit with the legs straight in front of you, knees facing the ceiling. The feet should be flexed and parallel to each other, the hands just touching the floor. Keep your back straight but your buttock muscles relaxed.

A First, simply tighten your buttock and leg muscles.

C Next, push the energy through the legs, pointing the feet. Keep your legs turned out and your little toes close to the floor.

SP/A

B Holding the muscles tight, turn the legs out from the hips. Move from the hips first and try to touch the floor with your little toes.

Sickled foot wrong

Caution: Do not let the big toes come near each other except in the parallel position. In all dance training you should try to avoid a sickled foot (see left), except for the very few "toed in" positions.

Arm Exercises

We normally think of arms as appendages for doing things with – for touching, holding, picking up and so on. In dance, that function changes completely. Only in partnership are they used to touch or lift; the rest of the time they are treated as extensions of the back to help balance and support the body. They are also important in determining the shape of a movement, and as useful tools of expression. There is more than one way of lifting your arms. If you think of them as being long and sensitive, you can lift them easily and with a sense of floating. On the other hand, if you imagine them to be heavy, you will lift them with a great sense of effort. Try using both these sensations here, but remember always to keep your shoulders down.

Sequence 1 In four counts, lift the right arm up from SP to A. Take another four counts to return to SP through B. Repeat three times, before doing the same exercise with the left arm. Tempo: medium.

SP. A B SP x 4 (right arm). **A B SP** x 4 (left arm)

Sequence 2 In two set of four counts, proceed from SP to C to D then back to SP, using both arms simultaneously. In each position, the arms should always stay at the edge of your vision as you look straight ahead. Tempo: medium.

SP. C D SP x 4

A Pushing down on your right shoulder blade and leading with your right hand, lift your arm up in front of you in one long curve. Stop when your hand is directly above your forehead.

B Open the right arm out to the side, palm facing up. As it passes through the horizontal, rotate the arm so that the palm is facing your legs.

SP Sit with your legs crossed, your spine long, and both arms on a long curve down in front of you, palms facing in.

C Repeat the same action as in A, but this time, bring both arms up in front of you, middle fingers almost touching. Be even more careful not to lift the shoulders as you raise your arms.

D Open both arms out to the sides, rotating them at the same time (as in B). Be careful not to force the arms too far back – they should always be within your field of vision.

Side Stretches

All dancers must acquire, and then maintain, a high degree of flexibility in the hip sockets. The more flexible you are, the easier it is to move. No matter how stiff you may feel, everyone is capable of improving their ability to stretch. All you need is the right mental approach and plenty of practice.

Side stretches should be long and sustained movements, performed without bouncing. Throughout the exercise, be careful to hold your knees straight and either facing the ceiling or slightly to the back. If they refuse to cooperate, try talking to them as you would to calm a nervous animal. It sometimes helps.

The Sequence Each change in your body must be motivated by the opposing movement in your legs. Taking eight counts to go between movements, exhaling slowly most of the time, stretch from SP1 to the right (A), curve over between the legs (B), stretch sideways to the left (C), and then in four counts, rise to SP1 by pushing down hard on the floor with the left leg and buttocks. Flex the feet (SP2) and repeat the whole cycle, but stretching over to the left first. The sequence finishes in the feet pointed position (SP1). Tempo: very slow.

SP1 A B C SP1 SP2 C B A SP2 SP1

SP1 Sit with your legs and arms stretched out to the sides, feet pointed and palms facing upward.

SP1

A

C

B

C Stretch to the left by pushing out through the right leg and opening your right hip socket. Curve over sideways as in A.

A Stretch to the right by pushing out very hard through your left leg. At the same time, open your left hip socket and pull the whole left side of the body up and away from the left leg. Let your torso curve slowly over to the right, bringing your left arm up over your head and sliding your right arm out along your leg. Stretch as far to the side as you can, keeping the torso facing directly to the front.

B Change the sensation in the legs by pushing out and back in both thighs. The pelvis and lower back will be pulled up and forward, making the torso curve over to the front. Extend the arms out to the ankles, palms down.

SP2 Sit in an easy body position with a long spine, as in SP1, but feet flexed, not pointed. Your heels should be off the floor if your legs are fully extended. You will find that the sensations of pushing away through the legs are even more intense in the flexed position.

SP2

Parallel Leg Flexes

Most people pay hardly any attention to how their legs are working, assuming that all is well down there, just because they manage to get around. One of the advantages of parallel leg flexes is that you can actually watch your legs working and refine the way they are moving. As you build up a rhythm of flexing and pointing, try to isolate individual muscles and joints. Work them hard but with care, teaching the muscles to coordinate with one another. If you cannot sit up straight with your arms in front of you, support yourself with your hands by your sides, as in Leg Exercises (p.62).

SP Sit high on the buttock muscles, abdomen held in and up so that you can feel the movement in the hip socket when you flex the legs. Your legs should be parallel, knees stretched, and feet long and pointed. Hold your arms in front of you without leaning forward.

A Bend your right knee and flex your right foot at the same time, pulling the top of your thigh muscle out and up, and your toes hard back toward your shin. Your heel should stay in one place on the floor, and not slide back. Keep your left leg fully stretched and pointed, so that you experience two different sensations running through your legs.

Sequence 1 On a count of eight, starting with both feet pointed (SP), flex and point the right foot twice (A, SP, A, SP), then repeat with the left leg (B). Tempo: slow.

SP. A SP A SP B SP B SP

Sequence 2 On another eight counts, go between A and B, so that as you point the right foot, your left leg is flexed, and vice versa. Keep the leg movements smooth and continuous, so that you get used to moving them at the same time. Tempo: slow.

SP. A B A B A B A B

Sequence 3 For the third set of eight counts, proceed from position B to C, simply by flexing the right foot. Alternate between SP and C. Tempo: slow.

B. C SP C SP C SP C SP

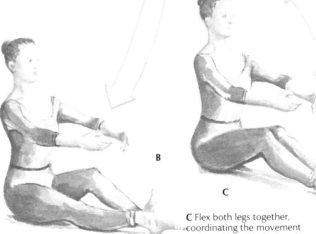

B Straighten your right leg and flex your left. As you straighten, use the buttock and hip muscles first, working down the leg until your knee is completely straight and your foot stretched forward.

C Flex both legs together, coordinating the movement in the ankles with the bend in the knees.

Kneeling Spine Curls

Kneeling on all fours, like an animal, is an excellent way of isolating the movement of the spine. This position allows you to work the spine equally between the arms and the legs. A frightened cat makes a perfect spinal contraction when it hisses and arches its back. Similarly, a wild horse bucks furiously to throw a saddle or rider off its back. Thinking of these instinctive animal movements will help you when you try this series of kneeling spine curls.

Sequence 1 Curl your spine (A) and release it (SP1) in four counts: contract 1, 2; release 3, 4. Start the release in the pelvis, so that you straighten the spine sequentially from the hip sockets. Repeat three times. Tempo: slow.

SP1. A SP1 x 4

SP1 Kneel on the floor, legs 3 or 4 inches apart and parallel. Lean over in one piece from the hips and put your hands on the floor. Bend your elbows slightly to bring the torso parallel to the floor. Your spine should have a saddle in it like a horse's back.

A Tuck your pelvis under by pushing down and tightening the muscles that run from your buttocks down the backs of your thighs. Pull up the centre of the spine, curving it as high as possible. Extend the curve to the neck so that your head tilts under.

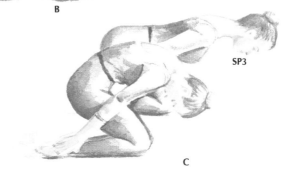

SP1

A

B Repeat the same movement as in A, but as you contract, try to get as much movement in the pelvis as possible. It will be more difficult to feel the backs of the thighs tighten because you are starting from a more stretched position, but with concentration and practice you should be able to get as much movement as before.

SP2

B

Sequence 2 Using four counts as in Sequence 1, repeat the same movements, but from the deeper starting position (SP2). Tempo: slow.

SP2. B SP2 x 4

SP2 Assume a deeper starting position by pulling your hips back and down so that your elbows are on the floor just in front of your knees. Make sure your spine is straight.

SP3

C

Sequence 3 The movement from SP3 to C and back to SP3 should take on a waving motion, with the head being left behind at the start of the contraction and then following through and scooping into the release. Repeat three times on a count of four. Tempo: slow.

SP3. C SP3 x 4

SP3 Kneel as in SP2, but extend both arms back along the torso, parallel to the floor. Stretch the spine forward, keeping your torso parallel so that the balance on the knees becomes precarious.

C Contract your spine up from the centre, keeping your feet on the floor, but pull back more on the legs than in B. Your arms can bend slightly, but the hands should stay back by the pelvis.

Rising from the Floor

After working on the floor for 20 minutes or more, you must make sure on rising that the legs are prepared to take your weight. Although you have been using your legs a great deal, you have not been putting your weight directly on them. Most of the time you have been stretching and this has a tendency to loosen the joints slightly. It is a good idea to train yourself to stay in control of your body in between exercises, rather than collapsing and letting go. For this reason, you should always rise from the floor carefully and with awareness, so that this transitional movement itself may become part of a dance.

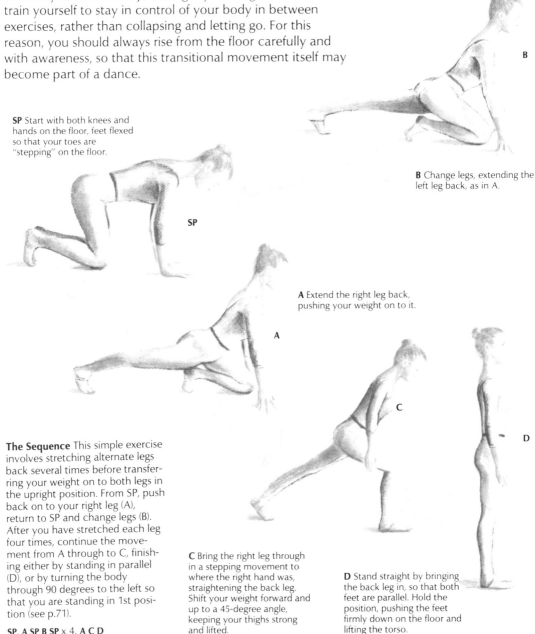

SP Start with both knees and hands on the floor, feet flexed so that your toes are "stepping" on the floor.

SP

B

B Change legs, extending the left leg back, as in A.

A Extend the right leg back, pushing your weight on to it.

A

C

D

The Sequence This simple exercise involves stretching alternate legs back several times before transferring your weight on to both legs in the upright position. From SP, push back on to your right leg (A), return to SP and change legs (B). After you have stretched each leg four times, continue the movement from A through to C, finishing either by standing in parallel (D), or by turning the body through 90 degrees to the left so that you are standing in 1st position (see p.71).

SP. A SP B SP x 4. **A C D**

C Bring the right leg through in a stepping movement to where the right hand was, straightening the back leg. Shift your weight forward and up to a 45-degree angle, keeping your thighs strong and lifted.

D Stand straight by bringing the back leg in, so that both feet are parallel. Hold the position, pushing the feet firmly down on the floor and lifting the torso.

CENTREWORK

After floorwork, you now get up for centrework – a series of exercises performed standing up in one place. Centrework is concerned with improving your posture or body alignment and with developing an awareness of your centre (see p.32). You will also be strengthening and improving the flexibility of your legs, and coordinating their movement with your arms. At first you may feel daunted at the prospect of doing so many things at once – developing good coordination, alignment and balance while moving between and holding positions. But just consider how many tasks we perform simultaneously without even thinking twice. We can walk and talk and carry a bag all at the same time and still not lose our way. Originally we learned to do all these actions one at a time; now we combine them into one, which we call "walking home from shopping". Learning the following exercises uses the same process. Once you learn how good alignment feels, you will be able to incorporate that feeling into your balance, then incorporate both sensations in a new idea of movement.

The Basic Positions of Dance

In order to exercise well, it is important to know exactly where your body is in a given space. The body positions shown here are basic to dance all over the world, because they are basic to our body shape and function. It is important to learn them well since it is easier to execute any movement with care and precision if you have a formal position to start from and return to. The positions known as 1st and 2nd can be done either with the legs turned out (as shown below) or with the legs parallel (as shown on p.72).

Turned out

Turned out

2nd position Expand your body to fill two-dimensional space: stand with feet apart, turned out and in line with one another, and arms held either down, as in 1st position (*right*), or out to the sides in 2nd (*left*). The palms may face down, forward or up – but in all cases, the arms should be held in a long curve out of the back.

1st position Stand in the shape of a figure one, with your legs turned out from the hips. Hold your arms in a long, shallow curve, palms facing slightly inward. Look straight ahead, keeping your spine and neck long.

3rd position One leg in front, heels and ankles just crossing, this marks the beginning of the body spiralling into space.

4th position Basic 4th extends the spiral forward, with one leg in front of the other, the feet separated by the distance you can stretch and point the front leg.

5th position Here the spiral is pulled tight, with the feet close to each other, front heel to back big toe, and hips and legs turned out to the same degree as the feet. Hold your buttocks in. The arms can be held up or down or in 2nd.

Basic Positions (continued)

All dance is based on positions and movement. Positions are places you start moving from, arrive at, or hold momentarily throughout a routine. The quality of the movement between the positions gives them their meaning. Positions are the body or substance of a dance. Movement reveals its soul.

Relevé in 1st This is another French derivative, from the verb *relever*, meaning to go up on to the half toe. A relevé can be done in any position, and infers that you are in such good balance that you can carry your weight on as small a surface area as the ball of the foot and toes. You may sometimes be asked to relevé on one leg.

Plié in 1st A plié is a bend of the knees, done with the legs turned out or in parallel. Derived from the French word *plier*, meaning to fold, it is commonly used in dance because it infers a whole quality of movement in the body, rather than a simple bend of the legs. The figure shows a half- or demi-plié, where the heels remain on the floor. Each knee must be directly over the middle toe, as detailed below, and not roll forward, pressing the arch into the floor *(below right)*.

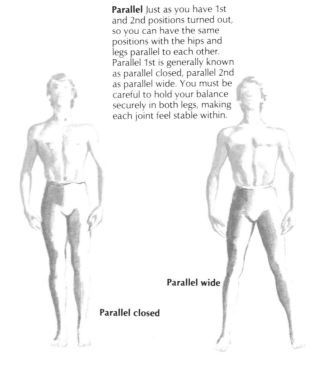

Knee over toes

**Wrong
Knee rolling forward**

Parallel Just as you have 1st and 2nd positions turned out, so you can have the same positions with the hips and legs parallel to each other. Parallel 1st is generally known as parallel closed, parallel 2nd as parallel wide. You must be careful to hold your balance securely in both legs, making each joint feel stable within.

Parallel wide

Parallel closed

Basic Positions (continued)

Here are some other fundamental positions that you can either hold or pass through. You should be able to recognize and remember them as they will help you to learn sequences of movement. Each position is one in which you can balance, either on the flat foot or the relevé (half toe).

Foot at ankle In dance, when you move one leg past the other, you should either bring it as close as possible, or keep it as far away as you can. Foot at ankle is as close as possible. Be careful not to twist the lifted foot in, like a sickled foot (see p.62).

Attitude One leg is lifted behind you, so that your body forms a long spiralling arc that runs from the back foot and out of the arms. You should feel as if your back ankle bone could sprout wings, like the Greek god Mercury.

Foot at knee Sometimes called passé or retiré, this position combines passing one leg close to the other with keeping the leg as high as possible. The toes should touch the inside of the standing leg. Do not lift your hip as you lift your leg; instead lift the weight up on the inside line of the standing leg and then transfer it to the centre of the body.

Arabesque Perhaps the commonest and most easily recognizable position, arabesque derives its name from the Persian design of a large teardrop. The lifted leg should be directly behind the other, with both legs equally turned out. Try not to lean forward, but hold the position strongly in the buttocks and shoulder blades.

Use of Parallel and Turn Out

As with any dance position, parallel and turn out convey an attitude of mind. A strong parallel position of the legs is usually associated with attack or defence, whereas the turned-out position implies vulnerability, exposing the "soft", unprotected parts of the body. Since you need to have a sense of physical strength when in a turned-out position, it is important to discover how to affirm the posture with your entire body. The movement should involve not only your legs and hips, but your whole upper body and even your face. If in parallel your vision is narrow, in a turned-out position it shifts to wide horizons, and you should feel like smiling.

SP Stand with your thighs, knees and feet facing directly to the front, your feet in line with each other.

The Sequence This exercise uses the large muscles of the buttocks and legs. Before moving your legs to turn out, feel your muscles tighten and turn around the pelvis. (You can experience this sensation more clearly if you practise the turn out beforehand lying flat on your back.) In five counts of two, proceed from SP to A, plié (B), point the right leg (C), then return to SP via A. Thus: turn out 1, hold 2; plié 2, hold 2; point 3, hold 2; close to 1st 4, hold 2; turn parallel 5, hold 2. Tempo: medium.

SP. A B C A SP

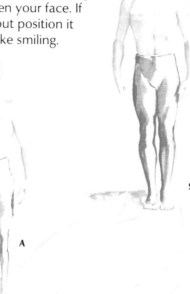

SP

A

A Turn your legs out from the hips, moving your muscles in advance of your bones. Avoid sticking your buttocks out by pulling up in the front of the hip socket.

B

C With a long stretching movement down the inside of both legs, rise from the plié and point your right foot to 2nd. The sole of the foot should slide along the floor.

C

B Keeping your heels together and your back straight, bend your knees into a demi-plié.

Parallel Exercises

Much of dance training consists of stripping away the acquired body attitudes and habits of movement and finding a new sense of balance based on your particular body proportions and a sense of your own centre and internal balance. Working in parallel means just that: your hips, thighs, lower legs and feet should be absolutely parallel to one another. Each of the following exercises – leg beats, pliés and contractions – should be performed with a strongly held parallel feeling in the body. Your focus should be straight ahead, and your body alert and ready for action.

Leg Beats

Although the exercise of stretching one leg away from you and returning it may seem simple, leg beats are practised by professional dancers every day in many different ways. These small movements may later be incorporated into larger patterns or dance steps.

Sequence 1 Using one count per beat, slide the right leg out from SP to A on one, close to SP and repeat for eight counts. Repeat with the left leg. Tempo: medium.

SP. A SP x 16 (8 each leg)

SP Stand in parallel position, arms down, knees facing straight ahead and the thighs, knees and arches of the feet pulled up.

A Keep both knees straight as you slide the foot out along the floor to point. The energy to stretch the leg should go down the back of the leg and under the sole of the foot. Pull up hard on the standing hip to keep it still.

B Slide the foot out along the floor, as in A, but continue reaching out until the leg comes off the floor, making a 45-degree angle. Keep the toes on the floor until they are as far away from you as possible. Raise the arms up to shoulder height, palms down.

C Slide the foot out, but this time lift your leg as high as possible, keeping both knees straight. Push down hard on the floor with your standing leg and lengthen the waist to hold the lower back still. Hold your arms up high to help feel the stretch in your torso.

SP

Sequence 2 Also on one count per beat, strike the right leg out to B eight times, returning to SP by touching the toes to the floor at the same spot (more or less) from which they were lifted. Repeat on the left leg. Tempo: medium.

SP. B SP x 16 (8 each leg)

Sequence 3 Essentially the same as Sequences 1 and 2, but this time strike your leg out as high as possible to C. Tempo: slow.

SP. C SP x 16 (8 each leg)

Parallel Pliés

All dance movements require you to bend and straighten your knees to some degree. Although bending the knees is not difficult, it is not so easy to do it smoothly and with controlled timing. It is even harder to do while controlling the posture and balance of the torso.

Sequence 1 In four counts of three, demi-plié to A (1,2,3; 2,2,3), then rise back to SP through B (3,2,3; 4,2,3). Do the exercise four times, then rest and repeat again. Tempo: fast.

SP. A B SP x 4

SP Stand in a parallel position, arms down, balanced evenly on your legs.

A Keeping the torso long and straight, bend your knees into a demi-plié. As you go down, raise your arms and lift up in your torso, as if you were lowering a large, precious bowl to the floor. Keep your heels on the floor.

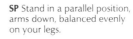

SP

A

B

B Start to rise up from the plié, using your arms to push against the space as if it were dense and difficult to move through.

C Bend your knees into a deep plié, taking as much weight off your legs as you can by holding the torso up and using the back muscles. Try not to lean forward or back, nor tilt your pelvis. Keep your heels on the floor for as long as possible; as you go down they will rise up naturally. Try not to sit on them at the base of the plié.

Sequence 2 Demi-plié twice as above, then plié again, but this time go all the way down to C. Do the deep plié in eight threes: four to go down, and four to come up. The heels should not come off the floor until the third three. Repeat the entire sequence again.

SP. A B SP x 2. **A B C B SP**

C

Parallel Contractions

A simple contraction, when added to the plié, will not only give you flexibility and strength, but will add a dimension of expressiveness to the torso. Remember that the contraction is a strong pull back and stretch of the spine.

The Sequence In four counts of three, proceed from SP to A to B and back to SP. Thus: contract 1,2,3; demi-plié 2,2,3; release 3,2,3; rise 4,2,3. Repeat. Tempo: medium.

SP. A B SP x 2

SP Stand in parallel 1st position, evenly balanced on the feet and legs, arms down. Without holding your weight forward, be ready to pull the back into the contraction.

SP

A

B

B Release by straightening the spine, starting with the pelvis and working up. Turn the arms, elbows down and palms slightly to the front. Complete the entire release before rising from the demi-plié position. To rise to SP, push down on the floor through the legs. Bring your arms down using your underarm and back muscles.

A Start the contraction before you plié. Tilt the pelvis under and up into the thighs, pulling the thigh muscles up and out of the knees. At the same time, curve the spine out to the back, starting as low as possible and working up the vertebrae in sequence. As the contraction reaches the upper vertebrae between the shoulder blades, turn the palms out and lift your arms up in front, leading with your elbows. Meanwhile, the upward pull in the knees should cause them to bend in a demi-plié.

Turned Out Exercises

The turn out is an exaggerated position, but one that is absolutely necessary for most dance training. It is necessary because of the way the top of the thigh bone fits into the hip socket, and because it gives you the strength needed for balance. At first, the turned out position may feel unnatural and restrictive, but once learned, you will find that it facilitates movement, especially to the side and back. The turned out exercises that follow will not only help reinforce this basic position, but also strengthen your legs and arms, and improve your coordination and sense of balance.

Sequence 1 Starting with the right leg pointing in 2nd (SP1), beat the leg into 1st position (A) and then back out again (SP1) in one count. Do 16 beats in this way, and then change sides in four counts through 1st position plié (T). Repeat on the left side for a further 16 beats before changing back to the right side. Do the entire sequence twice. Tempo: fast.

SP1. A SP1 x 16 (right leg) **T**
SP1. A SP1 x 16 (left leg)

Sequence 2 This is the same as Sequence 1, but beat the leg about 6 inches off the floor (SP2).

SP2. A SP2 x 16 (right leg) **T**
SP2. A SP2 x 16 (left leg)

Leg Beats

Leg stretches from 1st to 2nd position are movements that make you more aware of the mobility in your hip sockets, and thus help you to move the legs in isolation from the torso. By increasing your sensitivity toward the individual muscles of your legs and feet, these exercises will also make your legs stronger and more versatile.

SP1 Standing in 1st position, slide the sole of your right foot along the floor, as far away from you as possible, keeping the knee straight. Only the ends of your toes should be left touching the floor.

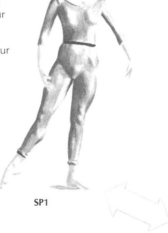

SP1

A

T

SP2

A Close to 1st position by sliding your foot back along the floor. Keep both legs, from the thighs down, equally turned out.

SP2 Repeat the movement described in SP1, but this time lift the right foot about 6 inches off the floor. Try to lengthen your leg as you lift it, keeping the hip bones level with each other. Keep your balance inside the body, not outside it – holding your arms in a long curve from deep in your back will help keep you steady.

T (transition) To change leg beats from right to left (and vice versa), go directly from SP1 or SP2 into 1st position plié. As you rise from the plié, slide your left foot out to SP on the other side, and repeat the sequence.

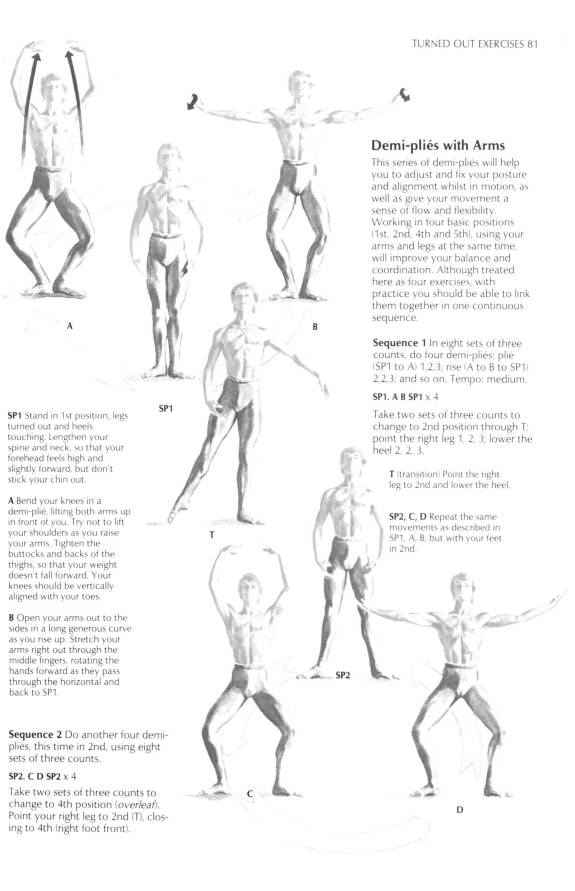

Demi-pliés with Arms

This series of demi-pliés will help you to adjust and fix your posture and alignment whilst in motion, as well as give your movement a sense of flow and flexibility. Working in four basic positions (1st, 2nd, 4th and 5th), using your arms and legs at the same time, will improve your balance and coordination. Although treated here as four exercises, with practice you should be able to link them together in one continuous sequence.

Sequence 1 In eight sets of three counts, do four demi-pliés: plié (SP1 to A) 1,2,3; rise (A to B to SP1) 2,2,3; and so on. Tempo: medium.

SP1. A B SP1 x 4

Take two sets of three counts to change to 2nd position through T: point the right leg 1, 2, 3; lower the heel 2, 2, 3.

> **T** (transition) Point the right leg to 2nd and lower the heel.

> **SP2, C, D** Repeat the same movements as described in SP1, A, B, but with your feet in 2nd.

SP1 Stand in 1st position, legs turned out and heels touching. Lengthen your spine and neck, so that your forehead feels high and slightly forward, but don't stick your chin out.

A Bend your knees in a demi-plié, lifting both arms up in front of you. Try not to lift your shoulders as you raise your arms. Tighten the buttocks and backs of the thighs, so that your weight doesn't fall forward. Your knees should be vertically aligned with your toes.

B Open your arms out to the sides in a long generous curve as you rise up. Stretch your arms right out through the middle fingers, rotating the hands forward as they pass through the horizontal and back to SP1.

Sequence 2 Do another four demi-pliés, this time in 2nd, using eight sets of three counts.

SP2. C D SP2 x 4

Take two sets of three counts to change to 4th position (*overleaf*). Point your right leg to 2nd (T), closing to 4th (right foot front).

Sequence 3 Standing in 4th position, right foot front, do four demi-pliés using only your left arm to lift. Complete in eight sets of three counts. Then, taking two sets of three counts, change to 4th position (left foot front) by pointing your left leg to 2nd (T) and closing to 4th. Do another four demi-pliés, bringing your right arm up in front of you. Tempo: medium.

SP3. E F SP3 x 4 (right foot front) **T**
SP3. E F SP3 x 4 (left foot front)

Change to 5th position by pointing your right leg to 2nd (T) and closing to 5th (right foot front).

SP3 Keeping the legs turned out from the hips, stand in 4th, one foot in front of the other. Try not to swivel your pelvis. If the right foot is in front, the left arm will be slightly forward. Hold your right arm out in a long curve to help keep your balance.

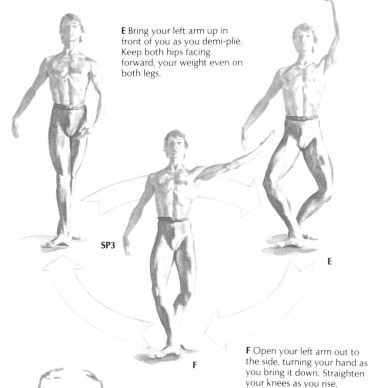

E Bring your left arm up in front of you as you demi-plié. Keep both hips facing forward, your weight even on both legs.

SP3

E

F Open your left arm out to the side, turning your hand as you bring it down. Straighten your knees as you rise.

F

Sequence 4 Using both arms on eight counts of three, do four demi-pliés in 5th, right foot front. Change to left foot front by pointing your left leg to 2nd (T) and closing to 5th. Do another four pliés in this position. Tempo: medium.

SP4. G H SP4 x 4 (right foot front) **T**
SP4. G H SP4 x 4 (left foot front)

SP4

G

SP4 In 5th position, the heel of one foot is placed beside the toe of the other. Feel your spine to be long and stretched, as in SP1.

G Lift both arms up in front of you and bend your knees, as in the previous demi-pliés.

H Rise from the plié opening your arms out to the sides. Bring your arms down to complete the movement back to SP4.

H

Pliés with Breath

One of the qualities we look for in a dancer is a sense of ebb and flow, a freedom of movement that comes from breathing well. If you are just beginning, you may find it hard to regulate your breathing to your movement. You will either be taking high short breaths or holding your breath. This could be due to not making full use of your rib cage when trying to hold a high position in the torso, or simply moving faster or slower than you can comfortably breathe.

In these pliés, you are going to control the timing as you breathe in and out, to produce a movement that has the quality of breath in it. The aim is to achieve a balance between breath and movement.

SP1 Stand in 1st, legs turned out, arms stretched out to the sides. Exhale.

C Inhale and relevé, holding the turn out. Raise your arms.

A Initiate the movement by breathing in. Plié, opening your arms out to the sides. Feel your back expanding into your arms.

B Continue inhaling as you deep plié. Don't sit on your heels – your weight should stay on your thighs. Raise your arms to counterbalance the lowering of your centre.

SP2, D, E, F Apply the same instructions as for SP1, A, B, C, but in 2nd position. Don't lift the heels up in the deep plié (E).

Sequence 1 Start in the exhaled position, SP1, then inhale and demi-plié (A) for two counts of three. Exhale in another two threes and rise to SP1. Repeat. Now take four threes to bend to deep plié (B), inhaling. Exhale and return to SP1 in another four threes. Repeat. Complete the exercise by inhaling and rising to the relevé (C) in four threes. Exhale and return to SP1 in four threes. Tempo: slow.

SP1. A SP1 x 2. **A B SP1** x 2. **C SP1**

Sequence 2 This is the same as Sequence 1, but all movements are in 2nd.

SP2. D SP2 x 2. **D E SP2** x 2. **F SP2**

Shifting Body Weight

All the work you have done so far has been on the spot. Although you have been moving a great deal, the movement has been around a still centre. New sensations will arise as you try to experience the feeling of moving in space while holding on to a sense of your own centre. As you shift your weight forward, remember that your alignment is held high in the torso, and that your head, arms and torso will change in basic opposition to your legs. (This means that if you step forward on your left leg, your right arm will move forward to the same degree.) Be careful not to sway or lean too far forward as you balance, but instead use your buttock and back muscles to hold you in place. Shifting body weight may seem a comparatively simple exercise, but it is the preparation for much bigger movements in space, such as running, skipping and leaping.

Sequence 1 In two counts, shift your weight from your right leg (SP) forward on to your left (A), and then forward again through B on to your right (C). Reverse the movement in another two counts by stepping back on to your left leg (D) and then back to your right (SP). Make sure you go fully forward with your weight before going back, and then go fully back before going forward again. Your knees will stay straight throughout except for the return through D. Repeat the exercise by starting with your weight on your left leg. Tempo: slow.

SP A B C D SP (right leg)
SP A B C D SP (left leg)

Sequence 2 As you become familiar with Sequence 1, try replacing A with a high leg lift, as shown opposite.

SP Stand back on the right leg and stretch the left out in front of you. Keep both legs turned out, and your upper body in opposition to your legs. Feel that your entire body is ready to move forward and up.

A With both knees straight, use your back and right leg to shift your weight forward on to the left leg. As you step, keep your turn out by pushing the left heel forward.

At the same time, move the right leg in a curve from the back out to point to 2nd position. Turn your face slightly to the right as you begin to change your arms.

B Continue moving the right leg until it finishes its semi-circular path to point in front of you. By now your left arm should be in front of you, mirroring the right leg.

C Continue the movement forward by stepping on to your right leg, holding the turn out. Stretch the left foot hard behind you and keep it pointing directly backward. Make sure your weight is fully on the right hip socket and the torso is held up.

D To return to SP, push back from the right leg and reach with the left foot behind you. Shift your weight back to the left leg and, at the same time, stretch the right foot out in front. Then bend the knee and bring the right foot to the inside of the left ankle. Complete the movement by stepping back on to the right foot. Stretch the left leg in front of you, ready to go forward again.

Contraction in 2nd

This is a strong activating contraction that produces a whiplike turn through the body and is used to motivate a movement in space. The "attack" to move starts in the torso with the pelvis tilting under, causing the spine to curve outward, and the arms and legs to turn inward. The same sequence of "attack" and follow through is repeated in the release, the second part of the movement. This is hard to perform at first without exaggerating and arching too far back. But with experience you will be able to feel the straightening or releasing of the spine very clearly. From the release you "unwind" the body back to the starting position.

The Sequence In two counts go from SP through T1 into the contraction (A). Take another two to release (through T2 and T3) back to the SP. The movement should be slow and weighted with a good sense of elasticity and pressure into the floor. Tempo: very slow.

SP T1 A T2 T3 SP

SP Start in 2nd position, arms and palms facing up, legs in demi-plié holding equal weight. Stretch your spine in both directions from the waist, so that the back feels long and free to move.

T1 (transition) The contraction starts in the pelvis. Tilt under and up into the hip sockets, curving the whole spine up to the neck. Rotate your arms so that the palms face downward.

T3 Keeping the same plié, turn your body out to the right by pulling your right leg back through 4th and out to 2nd. Your arms should start to open out to the sides. Control your "fall" back to 2nd by holding your pelvis strongly.

T2 Release the spine from the lowest vertebra in your back, pulling your weight straight back so you are slightly off-balance. Turn the arms to make the palms face each other and lift them up overhead as your shoulder blades resume their normal position.

A Pull back on the left side of the waist and, shifting your weight mostly to your left hip and leg, curl the whole right side of the body around to the left as if your body was folding in half. The spine pressing back and out between the shoulder blades should make the arms feel as if they want to turn in on each other, elbows bending up and backs of the hands facing each other. The same turning in sensation will happen in the legs. As the contraction goes up into the back of the neck, curve your head slightly over. Avoid bringing your upper body too far forward.

Jumping

One of the most exhilarating movements in dance, to do as well as watch, is flying into the air – leaping, skipping or jumping. As children we would frequently jump up and down just for fun. If you can bring some of that sense of fun to these jumps they will be much easier to do. In fact, if you are working with another person, it's a good idea to face each other while jumping. You will find that you help one another to keep going.

In order to coordinate all parts of the legs in preparation for jumping, you are first going to exercise the feet and ankles. This will also build up strength and warm up the muscles and joints you use for jumping.

Jump Preparations

Before you can jump, you must prepare your body. You have to build up strength in your feet, ankles, calves, thighs, buttocks and back. The following exercises not only strengthen these parts, but also develop coordination and rhythm in them, enabling you to perform a well executed jump.

Sequence 1 Starting with the right leg, go from SP to A to B and back to SP in one count. Do this eight times before repeating with the left leg. The movement to point (B) is on the "and" count, the close to SP is on the beat (*and* 1 *and* 2 *and* 3 etc.). Repeat on both sides twice. Tempo: medium.

SP. A B SP x 8 (right leg). **A B SP** x 8 (left leg)

Sequence 2 On four counts, plié (C), return to SP, relevé (D) and return to SP. Repeat seven times. Tempo: medium.

SP. C SP D SP x 8

Sequence 3 In direct imitation of the jump, without going into the air, plié (C) and relevé (D) eight times. Finish in the relevé and hold your balance. Tempo: medium.

SP. C D x 8

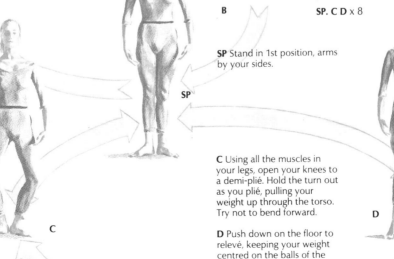

A Pull the muscles of the right thigh up and out to bend the knee, lifting the heel off the floor. Push the arch of the foot over the toes as far as it will go.

B Snap the right foot out off the floor by lifting the thigh and pushing off the floor with the toes. Pull your heel up toward your calf. Close to SP by pushing the leg down.

SP Stand in 1st position, arms by your sides.

C Using all the muscles in your legs, open your knees to a demi-plié. Hold the turn out as you plié, pulling your weight up through the torso. Try not to bend forward.

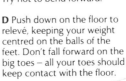

D Push down on the floor to relevé, keeping your weight centred on the balls of the feet. Don't fall forward on the big toes – all your toes should keep contact with the floor.

The Jumps

Use these jumps as strengthening exercises for more complicated air-borne movements that you can try later. When jumping, try not to hold your breath but breathe normally. There will be a tendency in both sets of jumps to "camel" the body – to rock the torso up and back in the air and forward on landing. Try to resist this by sustaining the long alignment of the spine throughout.

Sequence 1 Go from SP into the plié, A, and then jump continuously between A and B eight times with the beat on the landing. Each time you land, make sure you are in 1st position. Don't jump on your toes or bounce the heels off the floor – you will only strain your calf muscles. After the eighth landing, rise to SP1 and hold still. Repeat. Tempo: medium.

SP1 A. B A x 8 . **SP1**

Sequence 2 Before starting, repeat the plié relevé exercises (Sequences 2 and 3) on p.87, but with your legs and arms in 2nd (as in SP2) instead of 1st. The sequence of jumps will be as Sequence 1, i.e. do eight jumps going from C to D, finishing in SP. Do the sequence twice. Tempo: medium.

SP2 C. D C x 8 . **SP2**

After you have built up sufficient endurance, do 16 jumps twice with a short rest in between.

SP1 Stand in 1st position, feeling a strong internal sense of preparation for the jumps.

A As you demi-plié, check that your knees are turned out and aligned over the middle toes of your feet.

SP2 Adopt a 2nd position that you can hold strongly in the legs. Hold your arms out to the sides, palms up, elbows slightly higher than the shoulders and wrists slightly higher than the elbows.

C Plié, letting the knees extend slightly beyond the toes. Don't have your feet too far apart. The legs must be very elastic and should support the torso well.

B Jump up, making sure your feet point fully and snap up off the floor. Don't let them open too far – the effort must be straight up and not wasted with a kicking-out movement.

D Jump up by pushing off the floor, with the sensation that you are carrying your entire torso and arms up into the air. Your feet should be fully stretched.

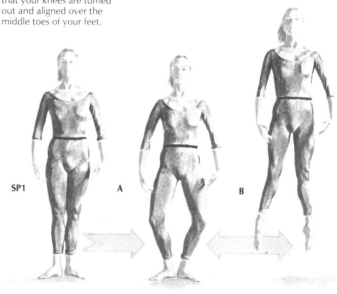

MOVING IN SPACE

Our bodies are designed to move in space. Urban lifestyles, however, are very restricting to our movements – many people sit in one place all day, and always go by car or take a train if they want to get somewhere quickly. Even when we go to a disco, we are often unable to move freely because of the crowds and so have developed a style of dance that allows us to move intensely in a very limited space.

In other countries too, dance forms have evolved in restricted spaces, making the feeling and movement of the dance more internal. Classic Japanese dance, for instance, is often done in one small square, while Spanish Flamenco has developed its inner intensity, its quick turns on one spot and strong floor accents as a result of similar space restrictions.

When it comes to dancing in space we need to retrain ourselves. All the work we did on centering seems to desert us when we try to move in space. But with concentration, we can overcome the feeling of being uncoordinated, and ultimately come to experience the remarkable sensation of being a beautifully organized and coordinated moving body.

Walking

To walk well is a dance in itself. Walking for exercise, with a springing step, arms swinging easily in opposition, head held high, legs taking long strides and moving quickly, is one kind of dance. Walking sensually, with long leisurely strides and exaggerated hip movement, is another. There are many examples. Indeed, the way someone walks is a barometer of their feelings or purpose. We frequently make judgements about people simply by the way they walk.

In dance, walking not only provides the linking steps but underlies all travelling movement itself, which is why dancers practise it so carefully. After all, running can be said to be fast walking, and a leap, the largest movement we can make, is the moment between two steps taken into the air.

Walking Practice

What is the first thing you do when you walk? If you thought it was to put out or move a leg, you are wrong. It is to shift the weight in such a way as to start the body falling off balance. You then catch it quickly with a leg. Walking is a series of falling and catching movements and how well we do it depends on how smoothly we can control the process.

Now practise walking, using the longest distance you can go in your space. Start off by walking in a free and easy rhythm to see how your body feels, and then try walking concentrating on different aspects of the body each time.

First, walk using your feet very hard. Imagine you are on a beach, throwing sand up behind you with your toes. Then walk making sure your knee is straight as you stride, and the head and torso are slightly in front of the pelvis. Now walk swinging your arms in opposition (see below). This may take some time. Finally, walk combining all these movements, holding your weight high in the pelvis and your spine stretched, in a continuous smooth flow through space.

The Sequence To step correctly from one leg to the other (R to L to R etc.), follow steps T1 and T2. These are not "steps" in themselves; they merely show you how to proceed between steps. In four sets of four counts, do 16 steps, leading off with the left leg. Start again, leading off on the right. Repeat several times. Tempo: slow.

R(SP). L R x 8 **L(SP). R L** x 8

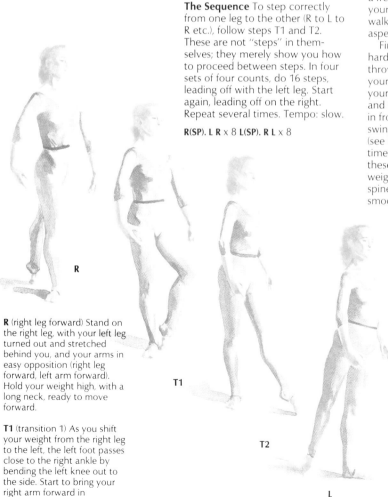

R

T1

T2

L

R (right leg forward) Stand on the right leg, with your left leg turned out and stretched behind you, and your arms in easy opposition (right leg forward, left arm forward). Hold your weight high, with a long neck, ready to move forward.

T1 (transition 1) As you shift your weight from the right leg to the left, the left foot passes close to the right ankle by bending the left knee out to the side. Start to bring your right arm forward in opposition.

T2 (transition 2) Continuing forward with the left leg, stretch it out in front of you, and bring the right arm forward to correspond with the left leg. Your weight should now be shifting to the left leg, giving you a strong feeling of pushing off from the right leg.

L (left leg forward) Take the weight fully on to your left leg, stepping on the outside ball of the left foot. Push the left heel forward to keep the turn out, and stretch your right leg behind you. You have now taken one step.

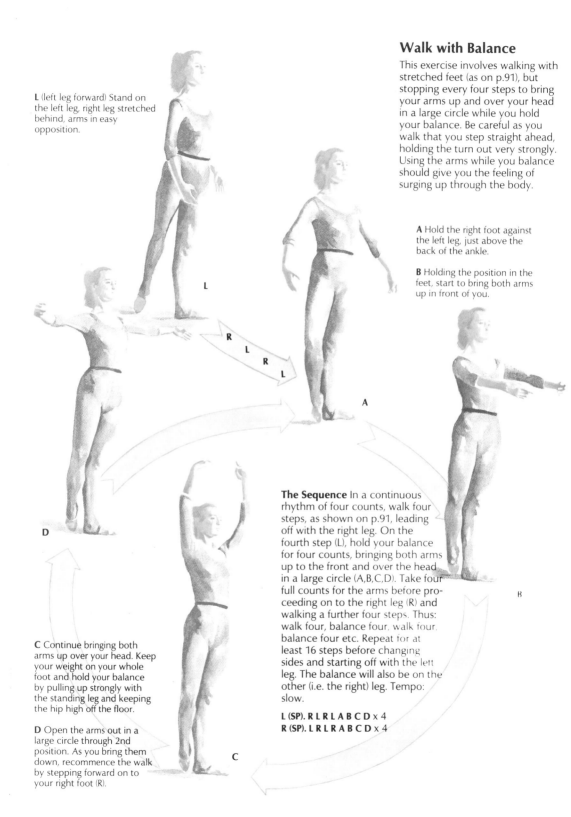

Walk with Balance

This exercise involves walking with stretched feet (as on p.91), but stopping every four steps to bring your arms up and over your head in a large circle while you hold your balance. Be careful as you walk that you step straight ahead, holding the turn out very strongly. Using the arms while you balance should give you the feeling of surging up through the body.

L (left leg forward) Stand on the left leg, right leg stretched behind, arms in easy opposition.

A Hold the right foot against the left leg, just above the back of the ankle.

B Holding the position in the feet, start to bring both arms up in front of you.

C Continue bringing both arms up over your head. Keep your weight on your whole foot and hold your balance by pulling up strongly with the standing leg and keeping the hip high off the floor.

D Open the arms out in a large circle through 2nd position. As you bring them down, recommence the walk by stepping forward on to your right foot (R).

The Sequence In a continuous rhythm of four counts, walk four steps, as shown on p.91, leading off with the right leg. On the fourth step (L), hold your balance for four counts, bringing both arms up to the front and over the head in a large circle (A,B,C,D). Take four full counts for the arms before proceeding on to the right leg (R) and walking a further four steps. Thus: walk four, balance four, walk four, balance four etc. Repeat for at least 16 steps before changing sides and starting off with the left leg. The balance will also be on the other (i.e. the right) leg. Tempo: slow.

L (SP). R L R L A B C D x 4
R (SP). L R L R A B C D x 4

Low Walk

This is a good exercise for experiencing a long, stretchy quality in the muscles. Basically, you repeat the same turned out walk with the foot pointing behind then coming past the standing foot, as described earlier, but this time you plié with the standing leg instead of holding it straight. Your head should be carried through space at a constant speed, not moving then stopping on each step. Let the whole movement be long and cat-like.

R (right foot forward) Start in a demi-plié on the right leg, the left leg stretched in a long line behind you. Both legs should be turned out and your arms held in opposition.

T1 (transition 1) As you shift your weight from the right leg to the left, the left foot passes close to the right ankle. Stay in low plié as you pass the foot through.

The Sequence Using a slower rhythm to make the movement more fluid and sensuous, practise the low walk moving from R to L to R. Take 16 steps in four sets of four counts, punctuating each beat with "and" to make the counting easier on the slower tempo (thus *and* 1 *and* 2 *and* 3 *and* 4). With each "and", you should be passing through either T1 or T2, depending on which leg you are stepping. Repeat the exercise leading off with the right leg. Tempo: very slow.

R(SP). L R x 8 **L(SP). R L** x 8

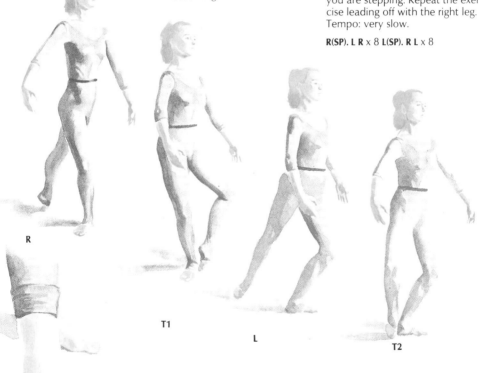

R

T1

L

T2

Holding the turn out To hold the turn out as you walk, step on to the outside ball of your foot first and push the heel forward as a separate movement before placing it on the floor.

L (left foot forward) Try not to drop down as you step on to your left leg, but keep the same demi-plié height from the floor all through the movement. Work your feet hard, stretching the back leg out behind you. Keep your spine long and upright, so that you don't lean forward over your front leg. Move your arms in opposition.

T2 (transition 2) Pass your right foot close to the left ankle as you continue the movement through to your right leg.

Triplet

Sometimes called a waltz step, a triplet is a travelling step on three counts, usually performed to a medium-speed waltz. A waltz is an easy rhythm to move to, distinguished by its bouncing triple time (1,2,3; 1,2,3 etc.). The accent is usually on the one.

If you don't have any waltz music, don't worry—you can still learn the triplet. Start by walking around your space in a large circle or oval, so that your movement is smooth and continuous. Count your steps in threes, keeping an even rhythm. You will notice that the "one" falls on a different leg each time. Continue walking in threes, but now try emphasizing the "one", so that your movement takes on an accent. Bend your knee on the "one", so that you make one down step and two up steps. All you need to do now is walk the up steps on your toes with stretched legs, as directed below, and you will be doing triplets.

The Sequence In a continuous count of three, step from SP on to the left leg (A) on 1, rise from the plié and relevé (B) on 2, and, holding the torso high, step through and relevé on the right leg (C) on 3. You then repeat the same movements on the other side (effectively reversing C and B). Try to keep the two relevé steps large and generous, so that all the steps in the sequence are performed with equal energy. After doing 12 triplets, start with your left foot forward in SP, so that you lead off with your right leg (D).

SP (right leg). **A B C D C B** x 6
SP (left leg). **D C B A B C** x 6

| SP | A | B | C | D |

SP Stand on the right leg with your left leg stretched behind. Hold your weight high in the torso, your head forward and up.

A In a long, low plié step, move the left leg forward, passing the left foot close to your right ankle. Move your right arm forward in opposition. Feel as if you are moving forward from the base of the spine—it will help you to keep your alignment. The step should be long enough to allow the right leg come off the floor behind you.

B Continue the forward movement, lifting your torso up and bringing the right leg through. Step with the leg straight and in relevé. Bring your left arm forward as you move.

C Keeping both legs straight and your weight high, step through on to the left leg in relevé, moving your right arm forward in opposition.

D Continue the next triplet by bringing the right leg forward in a long, low plié step, as in A, but on the other side.

Skips and Leaps

When you watch dancing, there seems to be an endless variety of movements into the air – jumping, leaping, skipping, hopping, galloping, etc. But in reality, because of your body's shape and function, the actual number of movements you can make is relatively small. The endless variety lies in the numerous ways you can perform these movements and put them together. Different combinations of angle, attack, bending or straightening the knees, or turning in the air, as well as the timing, can change the entire quality of a movement.

Movements into the air are either done on the spot, as in jumping and hopping, or involve travelling through space, as in skipping and leaping. For a skip, you jump off and land on the same leg. For a leap, you transfer your weight from one leg to the other, taking off and landing on different legs.

The Skip

As a child, you probably skipped quite often. Now, just to get used to the idea again, skip around the room in any way that feels comfortable. You will most likely skip from one leg to the other. Try to skip lifting the same leg each time, so that you step in between skips. That is the way we are going to skip here.

A Shift your weight forward on to your right leg, bending your right knee.

B Run forward on to your left leg. Swing your right arm down and up in front of you, and your left arm down and out to your left side.

C Bring your right leg forward, bending the right knee and lifting the thigh high up in front. Start to change your arms in opposition, swinging your right arm down and out to the side, and your left arm down, ready to move forward.

SP Stand on your left leg, with your right leg pointing in front of you, and your arms in opposition.

The Sequence Keeping a continuous rhythm of two counts, skip first on the right, starting with the left leg back (SP). Step forward (A) on count one, then (all on count two) step forward again (B), bring your knee up (C), skip (D) and land (E). Repeat five times, moving off on A, then do six skips on your left, starting with your right leg back. Tempo: fast.

SP. A B C D E x 12 (6 each side)

D Push *hard* off your left leg into the air, stretching the foot. Hold your right leg at right angles to your body, with the foot pointed and aligned with the knee. Swing your left arm forward and your right arm up and out to the side, keeping them both steady. Hold your shoulders down, and your head high.

E As you land on your left leg, cushion your weight, allowing it to come down and forward by using a very strong left thigh. Then hold your weight up in the torso. Your right leg should be ready to move forward and take your weight again (position A).

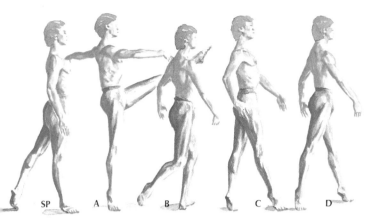

SP Start with the left leg back, ready to go forward.

A Swing the left leg through and up into a strong, straight leg beat. Eventually, this will be the leading leg in the leap.

B Plié as you step forward on to your left leg, cushioning the weight through your foot, ankle, knee and hip.

C Bring your right leg forward in relevé, lifting the torso.

D Keeping both legs straight, step through on to the left leg in relevé.

Leap Preparations (above)

In preparing to leap, you will be inserting a high leg beat (later a leap) into the triplet (see p.94) between counts three and one, as you go from the relevé to the plié.

The Sequence (above) Start the counting on "three" instead of "one" to get going. Thus, from SP, swing your left leg up (A) on 3, and then complete the triplet (B, C, D) on 1, 2, 3. The landing step (B) will always be on the first count, and the leg beat (A) will be on the third. From the relevé step, D, swing your right leg up (A) and repeat the sequence on the other side. Keep your back straight throughout the sequence. Do the exercise eight times. Tempo: fast.

SP. A (left leg up) B C D
A (right leg up) B C D x 8

The Leap (below)

When you leap you should feel your whole body stretching, as if to clear a fence. The leap itself consists of three parts: the take-off, the move through the air, and the landing. In addition, there are the ground steps, which differ from the leap preparations in two important respects: first, you don't relevé on steps two and three but do all the steps in running plié; second, *leap* on to the lifting leg, pushing off from the standing leg. When you land, you will still be in forward motion. Don't attempt to stay where you are but immediately transfer your weight forward into the next running step.

The Sequence (below) The tempo of this sequence depends on the elevation of your leap. The bigger the leap, the more time you will need between the counts. As in the leap preparations, you should alternate legs from one leap to the next. Thus, from SP, take three steps (A, B, C), swinging your leg into the air on the third count (C), leap, D, land, E, then repeat the sequence on the other side, counting the landing step (E) as step one. Leap four times.

SP. A B C D E A C (right leg up)
D x2. E

SP Start with your left leg forward, knee bent. Your right leg should be stretched straight back, and your arms held in opposition.

A Run forward on to the right leg, changing your arms.

B Continue gathering momentum as you run forward on to your left leg.

C Run on to your right leg and push down hard on it as you swing your left leg up.

D Leap into the air, transferring your weight forward on to the left leg.

E As you land, cushion the weight through the entire leg and hold your weight high to relieve the enormous pressure on the left leg.

Basic Workout Chart

This workout chart is designed to help you progress through the Basic Workout section. It lists all the exercises in order of appearance under three main headings – Floorwork, Centrework and Moving in Space. The Basic Workout session includes all the exercises and should take you about an hour from start to finish once you have learned the exercises thoroughly. For those of you who are just beginning, however, I have included a short workout session, which you should concentrate on first. It will give you a logical sequence of training that you should be able to master in a few weeks. As you gain confidence, add one more exercise to the short routine every three sessions, until you have learned the full basic workout.

You should aim to do a full basic workout *at least* three times a week. If you are pressed for time, don't skip a workout, do the shortened version instead. Dance training is a cumulative process – the more you work, the more you will learn how to work, and the more you will stand to gain.

FLOORWORK	SHORT	LONG
Sitting spine stretches	●	●
Breathing	●	●
Contractions		●
Leg exercises		●
Arm exercises		●
Side stretches	●	●
Parallel leg flexes	●	●
Kneeling spine curls		●
Rising from the floor	●	●

CENTREWORK

Use of parallel and turn out
Parallel leg beats
Parallel pliés
Parallel contractions
Turned out leg beats
Turned out demi-pliés
Turned out pliés with breath
Shifting body weight
Contraction in 2nd
Jump preparations
Jumps

SHORT	LONG
●	●
●	●
	●
	●
●	●
	●
●	●
	●
●	●
●	●
●	●

MOVING IN SPACE	SHORT	LONG
Walking		●
Walk with balance		●
Low walk		●
Triplet	●	●
Skip	●	●
Leap		●

Basic Dance Sequences

Since most dance exercises consist of dance material broken down into fragments and put into a repeatable form, you should be able to take those same exercises and link them together again into combinations which are like short dance phrases. Usually in a dance there will not be as much repetition as in class combinations, but as you progress, you can make up your own combinations out of the work you need to practise.

There are some simple rules you need to bear in mind when working through combinations:

1. The basic pulse should always be steady. Even if you change the counts from slow twos to fast threes, the rhythm should always be in multiples of the basic pulse.

2. Don't lose beats in transitions by not counting. Take your time on transitions, counting all the while.

3. Always shift your weight logically, even if you have quick changes of direction. You can bend a knee or use your torso in a different way to make a transition smoother.

4. Devise the combination, write it down and *learn it*. It is better that you do a short combination well rather than a long one badly.

The Combination I shall describe a combination made up of several exercises you have already practised. If it seems rather long to do all at once, try doing it in sections, practising each part alone. When you know the combination well, you may feel like rearranging it.

The combination consists of Walks with Balance (p.92), Triplets (p.94) with Skips (p.96), Low Walks (p.93), Contractions in 2nd (p.86), Jumps in 1st and 2nd (p.88), Triplets (p.94) and Leaps (p.97). Start in one corner with as much space in front of you as possible. Stand on your left leg with your right leg back and walk four steps, taking three counts for each step. On the fourth step, stay on your left leg and balance, while lifting your arms for four more threes. Then, starting with your right leg, do two triplets and one skip three times in a large semi-circle to your right,

alternating sides each time, so that you finish in the starting position. This will take three sets of three threes (two threes for two triplets and one three for the skip, three times).

From the third skip, step immediately on to your left leg and do six steps in the low walk toward the centre of your space. Take three counts for each step. On the sixth step, turn your body slightly left and end in 2nd position, ready to do three contractions in 2nd. The first contraction will be to the left, the second to the right, and the third will be to the left again. Take three counts to contract and three to release, making six threes in total.

Keeping the same pulse, change the count to twos for the jumps in 1st and 2nd. From 2nd position, you are going to jump to 1st to 2nd to 1st to 2nd etc. for six twos. Thus you will jump up on the last "three" of the previous sequence and land in 1st position plié on the "one". Each jump and landing will take one set of twos; on the sixth two, you will land in 2nd position plié, then shift your weight on to your left leg and rise up in arabesque on the "two".

Changing the counts back to threes, now take four triplets (starting with your right leg) curving in a large semi-circle to your left, so that you return to your starting point. On the "three" of the fourth triplet, brush your right leg through into a leap. Then go on to do four alternating leaps diagonally across the floor in another four threes, thus completing the exercise. The tempo of the whole combination will be determined by the speed with which you leap. Do try to leap on a slightly faster three-count than you would normally attempt – it will make the rest of the combination so much easier to do.

The Development Workout

Most dance exercises can be developed or made more advanced by the addition of new, more difficult steps or movements. In this workout, you will find both exercises you recognize from the Basic Workout and some entirely new material.

Of the Basic Workout exercises, you will see that some have developed in form, by which I mean the basic movements have become more complex or physically more demanding. In order to do them properly, you need to have learned the basic exercise well enough to do in your sleep – well enough to do without having to think about what comes next or what count you are on, well enough to concentrate solely on how you are doing the exercise, not on what you are doing. These development exercises also demand more physical strength than the basic ones. Muscle strength is by no means the only factor here – it is also a matter of coordination and balance.

Other basic exercises found here are a development in the sense of extending an implied movement out into the arms and legs and on into space. What in the Basic Workout seemed a small beginning now provides the starting point for an entire sequence.

In the Development Workout you will also find some entirely new exercises. As with any new material, you should take your time working out exactly how each sequence goes. It is far more important to learn the pattern carefully than to try to rush into doing a long sequence half-right. Your body learns mistakes just as it learns correct patterns and once imprinted on your muscular memory, mistakes are hard to change.

It is difficult to give any exact guidelines on when you should start to introduce the development exercises into your Basic Workout, because of individual variation in ability and experience. It takes about 30 repetitions of a sequence done well before it becomes really familiar to your body. Once you truly feel that you have accomplished that with the basic exercises, you can begin to incorporate the development exercises that lead on from the basics. Introduce them one at a time, repeating each new exercise over several sessions before you introduce another one. Finally, introduce the exercises that are entirely new, one at a time. Remember, there is no need to rush.

Bad basic training in dance is one of the most difficult problems that professional schools have to deal with. Often students try to advance too quickly. To train well takes years of painstaking basic work under the watchful eye of a good teacher, whereas students want to be challenged and inspired and learn to do advanced work right away.

It is hard to keep your enthusiasm and imagination alive doing the same exercises day after day, but that is the real challenge. To be able to practise the Basic Workout with concentration and authority, adding some development material from time to time, is far more important than trying to progress too rapidly.

The material in the Basic and Development Workouts is by and large the same work that members of the London Contemporary Dance Theatre did daily for years and years. It is a strange anomaly that the more advanced professional dancers become, the more important the basic work of dance becomes to them. In essence, you will get out of a dance training just what you are prepared to put into it.

FLOORWORK: Contractions

The seed movement, the very beginning of a contraction, can make the body move in a multitude of different ways, depending on how you attack and follow the impulse through into the torso, arms and legs. In this exercise, you start with the arms in a different position from the basic exercise (see p.60), and as you contract, there is a deep, flowing movement out into your arms and legs. You return by releasing your spine and drawing the movement back into yourself. It is a beautiful exercise for understanding and developing a sequence of movement that starts from the tiniest of impulses, and yet so energizes the body that it creates the movement itself.

The Sequence This exercise is in two counts of three: three to contract (SP to A through T1) and three to release (B to SP through T2). Hold position B for the first count of the release, and check that you keep your back straight as you return to SP. Repeat three times. Tempo: slow.

SP. T1 A B T2 SP x 4

SP Sit with your legs crossed and your arms held in front of you at shoulder height, elbows bent in. Clasp your hands together.

T1 (transition) Start the contraction in the pelvis, tilting the pelvis under and curving the spine up toward the neck. Push down into the legs, and as the contraction deepens, tilt the torso back slightly so that you are looking up at the ceiling. Extend the arms up, bringing the elbows together, and start to stretch the legs out.

T2 Continue the return back to SP by bringing the arms down, bending them at the elbows. Bend your knees as you bring your legs in.

B Release the spine, straightening up from the pelvis. Extend your arms up, keeping your legs straight.

A Complete the contraction by bringing the arms down and stretching them straight out in front of you. Your legs should be turned out and fully extended just off the floor.

Leg Exercises

To be able to hold your turn out while working, you have to train your muscles to rotate *outward* on the bones of your legs. In most people, the thigh muscles tend to pull in slightly toward the inside of the bones – especially in those who have not done much physical exercise. A simple way of finding out if this is the case with you is by observing your feet – if the arches fall in even slightly, the leg muscles are sure to be rotating in. These leg exercises are good for discovering whether or not you can achieve this outward rotation, as you can watch your legs carefully throughout.

Sequence 1 In eight counts, starting at SP1, extend the leg (A) 1, 2, 3; point (B) 4; flex (A) 5; return (SP1) 6, 7, 8. Repeat with your left leg, then do the whole sequence again. Tempo: medium.

SP1. A B A SP1 (right leg) **A B A SP1** (left leg) x 2

Sequence 2 This exercise is the same as Sequence 1, except for the position of your arms. Hold your right arm out to the side throughout the flex and point, returning it to the overhead position only as your leg returns to SP2. Repeat on the left side.

SP2. C D C SP2 (right leg) **C D C SP2** (left leg) x 2

SP1 Sit up straight with your legs bent up, as if in a deep 1st position plié. Step on the balls of the feet, pushing your ankle bones up to the ceiling and your knees down. Brace your arms on the floor.

A Lift the right leg just off the floor, increasing the rotation outward in the hip socket and outer thigh. Keeping the foot flexed and turned out, extend the leg straight out, lifting the heel flat up to the ceiling.

B Point your right foot, fanning the toes out and stretching the little toe toward the floor.

SP1

A

B

SP2

C

D

SP2 Assume the same position as SP1, but hold both arms overhead. At first it will be very difficult to sit upright.

C Extend the right leg forward, as in A, working hard to bring your pelvis up and forward against the turn out of the thigh. Open your right arm out to the side, pushing down on the right shoulder.

D Point your right foot, stretching right through to your toes. Imagine that your torso is pressing forward into your right leg. Hold the right arm out to the side.

Heel in Hand Stretches

Even if you are naturally flexible, it is important that you do stretching exercises regularly in order to counteract your body's tendency to tighten up as you strengthen the muscles. How far you can stretch depends very much on your mental attitude. Some people can practise stretching for years without actually improving, simply because they have a fixed idea of the limit to which they can stretch.

Heel in hand stretches are ideal for loosening and lengthening tight muscles. As you stretch, try talking to your body, coaxing it to let go a little more each time you work out. Feel yourself curving into the stretching parts of your body with an easy, flowing sensation.

Sequence 1 Proceed from SP through A, B, C, D and E back to SP in three counts of eight. For the first eight, bring your right foot up to the left knee (A) 1, 2, 3; contract your spine 4; grasp your foot and bring it to your mouth (B) 5, 6, 7, 8. The second eight is for the release (C, D): release and open your leg to 2nd 1, 2, 3, 4; let go of your foot 5; hold your leg up in the air 6, 7, 8. The third eight is to lower your leg back to SP through E, stretching the legs and spine. Repeat, then change sides and do the sequence on the left side twice. Tempo: slow.

SP. A B C D E SP x 4 (2 each side)

SP Lie on the floor on your back with both legs fully extended, turned-out feet pointed, right on top of left in 5th position. Stretch your arms out to the sides in 2nd.

E Now slowly bring the right leg down by stretching it out on a long arc away from the body, turned out and just off the floor.

A Slowly bend the right knee, bringing the right foot to the inside of the left leg just above the knee. Keep both legs equally turned out from the hips.

B Contract your spine so that your body is like a half-shell. Bring the left hand to the left hip and the right inside ankle bone toward your mouth. Take the right heel with the right hand and continue the movement toward your face.

C Start to release your spine, moving the left arm back out to 2nd and opening the right leg out to high 2nd position.

D Straighten the left leg as you stretch the right leg out. Your back should now be straight. Let go of the right foot and try to hold the right leg up in the air unaided.

Sequence 2 This exercise is in four counts of eight. On the first two eights, curve over (SP to A) and return back to SP. On the third eight, bring foot to mouth (SP to B) 1, 2, 3; flex (C) 4; point (B) 5; and lower the foot (D) 6, 7, 8. For the fourth eight, extend the leg (E) 1, 2, 3; flex (F) 4; point (E) 5; bring foot to mouth (G) 6; and lower back to SP 7, 8. Repeat, and then change to the left side (T1, T2, T3) in four counts. Do the exercise twice using your left leg. Tempo: slow.

SP. A SP B C B D E F E G SP x 2 (right leg) **T1 T2 T3 SP. A SP B C B D E F E G SP** x 2 (left leg)

SP Sit on the floor, with both legs extended to 2nd position. Keeping the weight equal on both sitting bones and your back straight, bend the right leg at the knee and bring the heel in as close to the body as is comfortable. Place your right hand, palm down, on your foot, between your ankle bone and heel, thumb around the Achilles tendon and fingers under the sole. Extend the left arm along the left leg. Breathe in.

T1 (transition) To change to SP with the left leg bent, move your right leg out to 2nd position, keeping both feet pointed. Raise your right arm up in front of you.

SP

A

A Exhale and drop forward, curving the spine over so that the top of your head touches the back of your right hand. Flex your left foot.

B With your right hand and arm, lift the right foot as close to your mouth as possible, curving your spine out to the back. Point both feet and keep the right knee bent and extremely turned out.

C At the highest point of the lift, flex both feet.

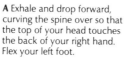

B

C

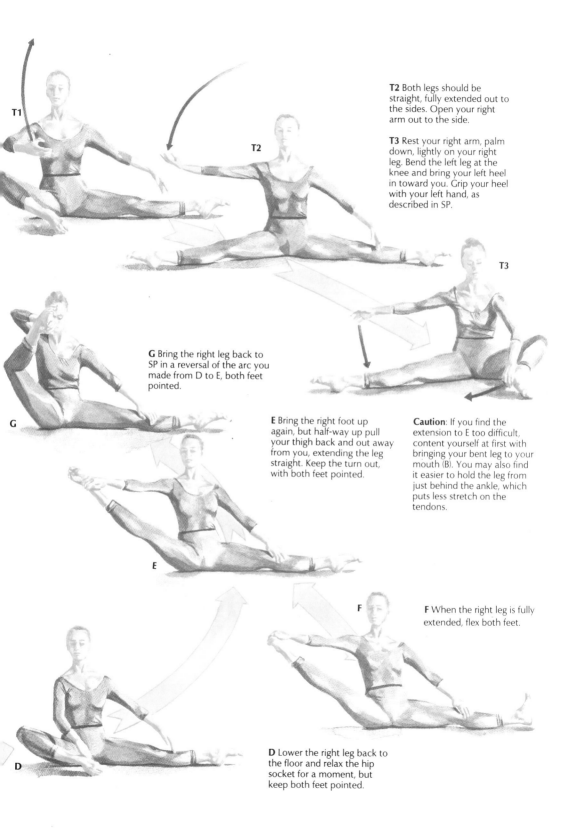

T2 Both legs should be straight, fully extended out to the sides. Open your right arm out to the side.

T3 Rest your right arm, palm down, lightly on your right leg. Bend the left leg at the knee and bring your left heel in toward you. Grip your heel with your left hand, as described in SP.

G Bring the right leg back to SP in a reversal of the arc you made from D to E, both feet pointed.

E Bring the right foot up again, but half-way up pull your thigh back and out away from you, extending the leg straight. Keep the turn out, with both feet pointed.

Caution: If you find the extension to E too difficult, content yourself at first with bringing your bent leg to your mouth (B). You may also find it easier to hold the leg from just behind the ankle, which puts less stretch on the tendons.

F When the right leg is fully extended, flex both feet.

D Lower the right leg back to the floor and relax the hip socket for a moment, but keep both feet pointed.

Combination Flex and Point

In dance there is always something new to learn. These exercises combine strong muscular movements with a complicated arm and leg coordination. Before using your legs, experiment with isolating the large back muscles. Start with both legs bent and try tightening first the buttocks, then the large back muscles rising up out of the pelvis. As you send energy out into your thighs, you will find the impulse to straighten the legs irresistible. When you have mastered this exercise, you can begin to experience how the coordination of arms and legs emanates from your central axis. As you work, think of yourself as a sculptor, moulding, carving and refining your muscles into shapes useful for expression.

Sequence 1 On a slow count of eight, flex your right leg (A) 1, point (SP) 2, flex your left leg (A) 3, point (SP) 4, etc. As you straighten the legs, tighten your buttocks and extend the energy out and away from you. Repeat. Tempo: slow.

SP. A (right) **SP A** (left) **SP** x 4

Sequence 2 On another count of eight, flex and point both legs simultaneously four times (SP B SP B etc.). Repeat.

SP. B SP x 8

Sequence 3 Now try flexing the left leg as you straighten the right, and vice versa. Repeat.

SP. A (right) **A** (left) x 8

SP With your legs stretched out to the sides and a straight spine, sit in as wide a 2nd position as you can comfortably hold. Your arms should be held out to the sides, and your knees straight and facing the ceiling. Be careful not to let your knees roll in, or forward, nor your feet sickle (see p.62).

B Flex both legs at the same time, again without sliding your heels on the floor.

A Flex your right leg as far back as it will go without sliding your heel on the floor.

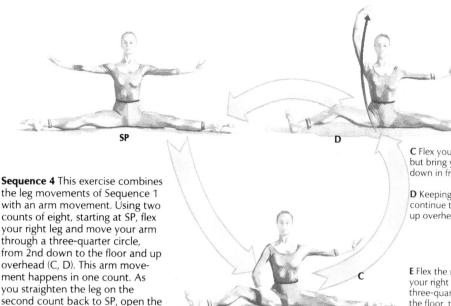

SP Sit with the legs and arms out to the sides, feet pointed.

Sequence 4 This exercise combines the leg movements of Sequence 1 with an arm movement. Using two counts of eight, starting at SP, flex your right leg and move your arm through a three-quarter circle, from 2nd down to the floor and up overhead (C, D). This arm movement happens in one count. As you straighten the leg on the second count back to SP, open the arm for the remaining one-quarter circle out to 2nd. Repeat on the left side for the next two counts, alternating between left and right until you have completed 16 counts. Tempo: slow.

SP. C D (right) **SP C D** (left) **SP** x 4

C Flex your right leg, as in A, but bring your right arm down in front of you.

D Keeping the right leg flexed, continue the arm movement up overhead.

E Flex the right leg and move your right arm through a three-quarter circle, down to the floor, then up overhead.

F Point your right leg and open your right arm out to the side in a quarter circle. Simultaneously, flex your left leg and move your left arm through a three-quarter circle (down to the floor then up overhead).

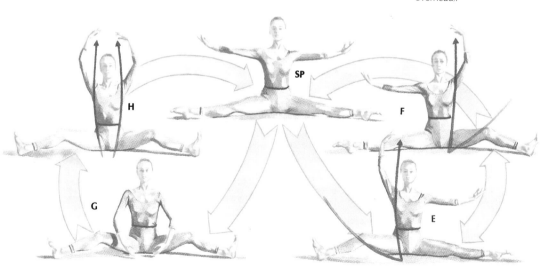

G Flex both legs and bring both arms down from the sides to the floor.

H Keeping both legs flexed, continue the arm movement by raising both arms overhead.

Sequence 5 This sequence is in two eights. For the first eight, you flex and point both legs (E and F) alternately, adding in the arm movements. You will find it difficult to do a three-quarter circle with one arm and a quarter circle with the other. For the second eight, you move both legs and arms together. Flex both legs and bring both arms down to the floor (G), then up overhead (H). Alternate between positions G, H (one count) and SP four times. Tempo: slow.

SP. E F x 4. **G H SP** x 4

Hip Spiral

The hip spiral is a specific exercise for developing the sensation of sequential movement through the body. It starts with the opening of the hip socket and works its way up the back, vertebra by vertebra, until it flows out of the crown of the head. The exercise also develops strength and flexibility in your back and legs and, more importantly, enables you to work clearly on the idea of isolation of movement. Although it is a series of movements involving the whole body, you should concentrate initially on isolating each movement to increase your awareness of the spiral. If you close your eyes while turning, and visualize the movement spiralling up your spine, you will discover a whole new world inside your body.

SP Facing right, sit with the left leg bent, foot flexed and stepping on to the ball of the foot, and the right leg bent back, foot stretched. Hold both arms in a long curve, left arm between your thighs, palm up, and right arm out to the side.

The Sequence This exercise is in six counts of three: turn to the front and lean forward (SP, A, B) 1, 2, 3; arch over to the elbow (C) 2, 2, 3; contract over (D) and return to the arched-sideways position (C) 3, 2, 3; repeat D and C 4, 2, 3; contract over (D) and swing round to the curved-over position (E) 5, 2, 3; release back to SP, 6, 2, 3. Repeat the sequence three times, and then do the exercise on the other side. Tempo: very slow.

SP. A B C D C D C D E SP x 8

E Swing the curved torso to finish curved over between the legs. Let the right arm describe a circle, fingertips just touching the floor, until it comes round to the SP. The left arm will follow suit.

A Open the right hip socket, turning your pelvis. Curve your spine, bone by bone, up to the head. Point the left foot and raise your left arm up over your head (now facing left).

D Start a twisting contraction by bringing the right shoulder and the left hip toward each other. Lift the centre of the spine upward and bring the right elbow and forearm down to the floor parallel to the left. The right ear will finish close to the floor. Pull the abdomen up away from the floor so that the back is curving as well as twisting.

B Lean forward toward your left leg. The left knee will come down to the floor, but the leg should stay strong and not feel crushed by the weight. Bring both arms down to floor level, palms facing up.

C Arch the torso to the left, sliding your left hand along the floor, elbow bent. Curve your right arm up over your body. The spine should make a curving bridge to the floor.

Side Falls

As dance is used to convey inner feelings and emotions, we have to find ways of expressing them through the body. Falling to the floor and its opposite, recovering and coming up again, are movements in dance which have been introduced out of expressive necessity. They are used to indicate inner feelings of "falling", such as "falling head over heels in love" or "falling into a deep depression".

The secret of falling well is to do it without hitting any protruding bones on the way down. As the floor is hard, all the "give" has to be in your body to make the movement smooth. Coming up again is a matter of being able to shift your weight logically so that you rise with ease and direction.

SP1

J Swing the torso back to the legs, first forward and then to the left, following with your arms to resume SP.

I To recover, bring the left leg down and in, and push down on the left hand.

H Flip your left leg up above you, extended straight and turned out, so that the knee is facing your head.

G Bring your torso down on to the floor, with your right arm fully extended, and your left arm bent at the elbow, palm down in front of your chest. The left leg should be stretched out to the left to balance the weight.

SP1 Sit on your right buttock, both legs bent at the knees to your left. Start with both arms held shoulder-high and out to your left. Feel the weight of your arms on your back so that as you move your back they will move too.

Sequence 1 Proceed from SP1 through A, B, C, D, E, F, G, H, I and J back to SP1 in three sets of three counts: swing the arms and torso in a full circle on the first three (SP1, A, B, C, D); slide out to the right and flip your leg up on the second three (E, F, G, H); and recover (I, J, SP1) on the third three. Repeat on the left side. Tempo: medium.

SP1. A B C D E F G H I J SP1

F Continue falling over to the right, so that your right leg is in full contact with the floor. Start to stretch your left leg out to the left side. Turn your face toward your right arm.

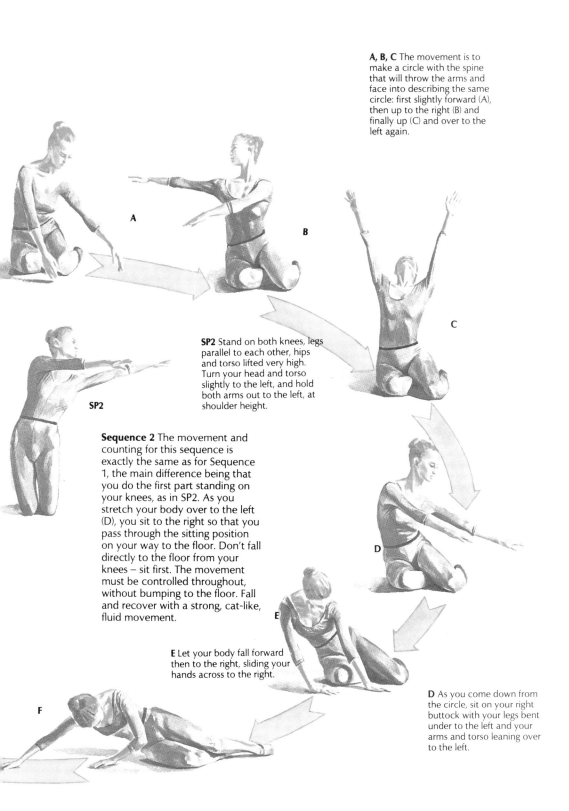

A, B, C The movement is to make a circle with the spine that will throw the arms and face into describing the same circle: first slightly forward (A), then up to the right (B) and finally up (C) and over to the left again.

A

B

C

SP2 Stand on both knees, legs parallel to each other, hips and torso lifted very high. Turn your head and torso slightly to the left, and hold both arms out to the left, at shoulder height.

SP2

Sequence 2 The movement and counting for this sequence is exactly the same as for Sequence 1, the main difference being that you do the first part standing on your knees, as in SP2. As you stretch your body over to the left (D), you sit to the right so that you pass through the sitting position on your way to the floor. Don't fall directly to the floor from your knees – sit first. The movement must be controlled throughout, without bumping to the floor. Fall and recover with a strong, cat-like, fluid movement.

D

E

E Let your body fall forward then to the right, sliding your hands across to the right.

F

D As you come down from the circle, sit on your right buttock with your legs bent under to the left and your arms and torso leaning over to the left.

Sequence 3 This exercise is a continuation of Sequence 2. You start on your knees, as in SP2, swing your arms (A, B, C, D), slide to the floor and lift your leg (E, F, G, H). But, in contrast to Sequence 2, you return not to both knees, but to your right knee and left foot (K). Rise up and balance in arabesque (L, M, N). Swing your arms (O, P, N) and slide back to the floor (Q, R, S). Return to standing by reaching up and balancing in arabesque again (K, L, M, N). Repeat on your left side. Tempo: medium.

**SP2 A B C D E F G H K L M N O P N
Q R S K L M N**

K Start the recovery by pushing down on to your right knee and left foot. Be careful where you place your left foot – if it is too far away from you, you will have to lean your upper body over to get up.

S Slide your torso down on to the floor, right arm fully extended, and flip your left leg up over you (as in H, p.118).

R Sit on the side of your right calf, sliding the leg slightly as you take your weight on it. Move your hands along the floor to your right.

Q Start to stretch back to the floor, keeping your weight on your left leg. Control your fall by pulling up and stretching your arms very strongly in the opposite direction.

L Continue pushing your weight over the right knee until you can rise on to your left leg.

M Take your weight on to your left leg and rise up, stretching your arms out.

N Balance in arabesque, lifting your right leg behind you, both legs turned out.

O, P Swing the arms in a full circle as you did on the floor.

Leg Lifts and Spine Stretches

These exercises use the floor as a brace to push against. They will seem difficult at first because you will have to keep everything under control with your face to the floor. You should concentrate on the sensation within the muscles and the internal correspondence between parts of the body to know where you should be in a position. In the leg-lifting exercise, for example, there will be a tendency for the leg to drift out to the side unless you ensure that it lifts straight up.

If you don't have a strong turn out, you may find the feet-flexed position too difficult to hold at first. In this case, point your feet, but be even more careful to hold the turn out in the leg that remains on the floor.

Sequence 1 (Leg Lifts) The exercise is in two counts of four: four counts to lift the leg (SP, A, B) and four to lower it back through A to SP. At the top of the lift (B), hold the position for a moment before bringing it down to the floor (A). Flex the leg (SP) before stretching and lifting the left leg. Repeat on each leg. Tempo: very slow.

SP1. A B A SP1 (right leg) **A B A SP1** (left leg) x 2

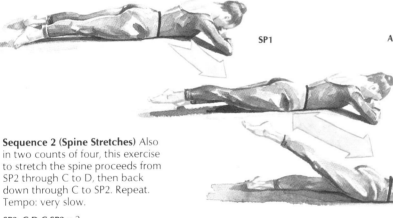

Sequence 2 (Spine Stretches) Also in two counts of four, this exercise to stretch the spine proceeds from SP2 through C to D, then back down through C to SP2. Repeat. Tempo: very slow.

SP2. C D C SP2 x 2

SP1 Start face down on the floor, elbows bent out, hands one on top of the other and forehead resting on the hands. Hold your legs turned out, feet flexed as if standing.

A Before moving, tighten the whole of your body. Pull the abdomen up and lengthen the spine into the legs and up through the neck. Increase the turn out so that your ankle bones are as close to the floor as possible. Start the movement by stretching the right leg more than the left and pointing the foot.

B Lengthening the underside of the leg, slowly lift the right leg as high as it will go. Feel the energy go down and out through the leg on a long curve up from the centre of the body. Don't shorten the lower back or clench your buttocks – they will tighten naturally. Keep the turn out in the left hip and thigh.

SP2 Place your hands palms down, alongside your shoulders.

C Stretch your feet, and with a scooping out and lengthening sensation through the head, push down on the hands, moving the energy through the front of the upper torso. Don't tighten the lower back, but try to keep the feeling of the vertebrae being open and well separated.

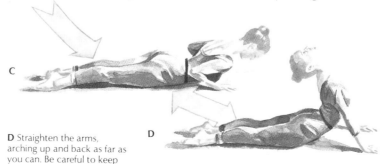

D Straighten the arms, arching up and back as far as you can. Be careful to keep your legs stretched.

Contraction Arches

In this sequence you will be moving from a release position on the floor into a sitting contraction, from which you will then push your body up into a high arch. Every move should be performed as efficiently as possible – it will help if you visualize each stage before you move into it. Lie on the floor, close your eyes, try to see yourself in the sitting contraction, then very quickly whip your body round into it. Do the same before the arch, making sure your feet and hands are correctly positioned to take your weight as you arch up.

SP Lie face down, with your feet pointed and parallel. Place your hands close to your shoulders, as if you were going to do a press-up.

A Tightening your entire body, stretch your right leg out and up behind you.

B Stretching from the hip, bend your right leg to a high turned-out attitude position, as if to touch your left shoulder with your right toe.

C Start to bring your upper torso up into a contraction, turning into your right leg and rolling over on your left.

SP

A

The Sequence Starting at SP, push yourself up in one strong move through A, B and C into a sitting contraction (D). Release up in another strong move to the high arch (E). Return to D by lowering yourself down, controlling your weight with your thighs. Take one more strong move to go back to SP through C, B and A, moving so tightly that as little of you as possible touches the floor. The exercise is on four counts: two to contract and arch up, and two to return. Do it four times on the right, and then four times on the left. Tempo: slow.

SP. A B C D E D C B A SP x 4 (right side). **A B C D E D C B A SP** x 4 (left side)

B

C

D

D Move swiftly into a sitting contraction, holding the right leg in close to you, foot flat on the floor, and stretch the left leg out, foot pointed. Tuck the right arm into your chest, fist clenched.

E

E Thrust your body up into a high arch, supported on three points – the outside of the left foot, the ball of the right foot, and the left hand. Push up very strongly through the right hip and extend your right arm up to the ceiling.

Kneeling Spine Curls

The development exercise of kneeling spine curls has a fluid, wave-like motion. It involves leaning forward in a contraction and then tilting the whole torso back and forward again on the release. You may find the movement a strain on your thighs at first, depending on your weight and the muscle strength in your legs. As you unfold your body, you can relieve some of the pressure on your thighs by holding more tension in your buttock and abdominal muscles. If it's too hard, don't go as far back at first, so that the torso is only at a 60- or 70-degree angle to the floor. Above all, be sure to resist relieving the weight by sitting back on your legs and pinching the knees.

The Sequence Use eight counts for this exercise, punctuating each count with "and" (*and* 1 *and* 2, etc.). Take four counts to contract to the tilted-back position (SP, A, B), and four to release back to SP (through C, D and E). Do the exercise four times. Tempo: very slow.

SP. A B C D E SP x 4

SP Kneel on the floor, legs 3 or 4 inches apart, with both arms extended back along the torso. Lean forward, stretching the spine and keeping your torso parallel to the floor.

A Take a deep contraction, turning the pelvis under and into the front of the hips and thighs. On the curl, let your face pass as close to the knees as possible.

B Continue unfolding the torso until the body forms a long, shallow curve, making a 45-degree angle to the floor. Keep the chin down and your hands just touching your heels. The pelvis should be the same distance away from your heels as it was in the SP. Try to hold your weight with your entire back, not just the thighs alone.

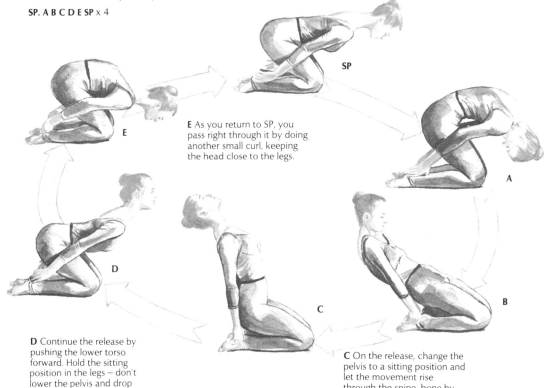

SP

E As you return to SP, you pass right through it by doing another small curl, keeping the head close to the legs.

A

D

C

B

D Continue the release by pushing the lower torso forward. Hold the sitting position in the legs – don't lower the pelvis and drop your weight.

C On the release, change the pelvis to a sitting position and let the movement rise through the spine, bone by bone, until the release lifts the face to the ceiling.

Rising from the Floor

Here you concentrate on building strength in your back and legs so that they are ready to take your weight as you rise up from the floor. Some of the movements are difficult, however, and should be tackled with care. In the first sequence you twist your weight from one side of the body to the other while maintaining an inverted "V" shape; in the second, you contract and release your torso, still keeping your hands and feet on the floor. In the third sequence, you touch your legs with your head, alternating between a bent- and straight-knee position until you finally rise to a standing parallel position.

Sequence 1 Positions T1, T2 and T3 do not qualify as full positions in this exercise; they are merely pre- paratory moves to lead you into the starting position (SP1). Run through them in your own time, holding the squatting position T2 for about 10 or 15 seconds before falling forward on to your hands (T3). The exercise is in eight counts, proceeding from SP1 to A on one, and alternating between positions A and B in a series of deep pressing movements up to eight. You should feel as if you are running on the spot. At the end of the sequence, return to sitting on your heels (T2) for another four counts. Tempo: slow.

T1 T2 T3 SP1. A B x 4. **SP1 T3 T2**

T1 Start from the hands-and-knees position, with the toes turned under.

T2 Using your hands, push your weight back on to the feet. Sit on your heels and relax your legs, pushing your body forward. Squatting in this way requires not only a degree of stretch in the Achilles tendons and lower back but also the ability to balance and coordinate opposing muscles and tendons.

T3 Fall forward on to your hands.

SP1 Straighten your legs and walk your hands away until you are in an inverted V position, with equal body weight on the hands and feet.

A Shift the weight in the legs and hips to take more on the right side, making the right knee bend, the right foot relevé and the right shoulder twist down. Try to touch the floor with your right elbow. Your chest will turn left.

B Shift your weight to the left side, mirroring the movements in position A.

Sequence 2 You will finish Sequence 1 in the squatting position, T2. Take four counts to move into SP2 by falling forward on to your hands, T3, and straightening your legs (SP2). Then in four counts of four (1, 2 to contract; 3, 4 to release), alternate between positions C and D four times. Return to SP2. Tempo: slow.

T2 T3 SP2. C D x 4. **SP2**

C Inhaling, tilt your pelvis and contract your spine, working sequentially up the back so that your head curves under.

D Exhaling, release your spine, stretching the backs of the legs and shoulders.

SP2 Fall forward on to your hands, keeping your legs straight, to assume an inverted V shape, as in SP1.

Sequence 3 Move into SP3 through T4 in two counts. Straighten (E) and bend your knees (SP3) four times in four counts of four (1, 2 to straighten; 3, 4 to bend). Then in free time, straighten your legs (E) and slowly rise to a standing parallel position (T5, T6, T7). Tempo: slow.

T4 SP3. E SP3 x 4. **E T5 T6 T7**

T4 Keeping your legs straight, walk your hands in toward your feet, compressing the inverted V shape.

SP3 Hold the backs of your heels with your hands, so that your forearms are resting against the backs of your legs. Bend your knees, keeping your head touching your legs.

E Straighten the knees. With your head and torso tucked in close to your legs, your whole body should assume a neat and compact shape.

T5 Let go of the backs of your legs and relax, allowing your torso to hang over.

T6 Keeping your arms relaxed and hanging down, slowly straighten your spine, working from the pelvis upward.

T7 Your spine fully straightened, stand in 1st position, legs parallel.

CENTREWORK: Parallel and Turn Out

This sequence adds an arm movement to the basic exercise (p.75) enabling you to work more deeply in the body. Before starting, try the following exercise to increase awareness in your arms. Stand in a doorway, arms by your sides and palms on your thighs. Open your arms straight out until the backs of your wrists press against the door jambs. Expand your back muscles outward and push very hard with both arms, keeping your elbows straight. Slowly count to ten, then relax your arms back down and step out of the doorway. Your arms should float out and away from you effortlessly. Do this several times, then try to imitate the sensation just by lifting your arms up in front of you. This exercise is important for experiencing how your arms should feel when you move them using muscle power from the back.

The Sequence Proceed from SP through A, B, C, D and E back to SP in five counts of two: two to turn out (A); two to plié (B); two to extend to 2nd (C, D); two to return to 1st (E); and two to finish in parallel (SP). Repeat three times, then do the whole sequence on the other side. Tempo: slow.

SP. A B C D E SP x 8 (4 each side)

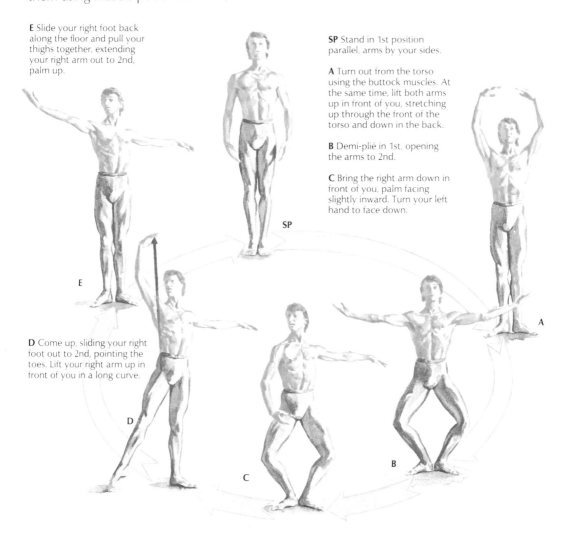

E Slide your right foot back along the floor and pull your thighs together, extending your right arm out to 2nd, palm up.

SP Stand in 1st position parallel, arms by your sides.

A Turn out from the torso using the buttock muscles. At the same time, lift both arms up in front of you, stretching up through the front of the torso and down in the back.

B Demi-plié in 1st, opening the arms to 2nd.

C Bring the right arm down in front of you, palm facing slightly inward. Turn your left hand to face down.

D Come up, sliding your right foot out to 2nd, pointing the toes. Lift your right arm up in front of you in a long curve.

Parallel Pliés with Contraction

Here you extend the demi-plié of the basic exercise (p.78) to perform a *deep* parallel plié, which makes both balance and alignment harder. In addition, you must now change the hold of your spine at the bottom of the plié from a contraction to a release. Be prepared to isolate your torso from your legs so that you can work them independently. Especially at the bottom of the plié, it will help if you visualize the way your body balances on the two tiny parts of your feet that are on the floor and yet is still free enough to move from the contraction to the release without altering that balance. On the plié, feel that you are pulling your legs up toward you, to keep the joints open and stretched and prevent your knees from closing up.

The Sequence Do two demi-pliés (as in the basic exercise, p.78), in eight threes before attempting the deep plié. Use eight threes for the deep plié: four threes to go down (SP, A, B) and four to come up (C, D, SP). Repeat the whole pattern. Tempo: fast.

SP. A D SP A D SP A B C D SP x 2

SP Stand in a carefully balanced parallel position, arms down by your sides.

A Start the contraction by tilting the pelvis under and up against the legs and pulling the thigh muscles up and out of the knees. As you curve the spine to the back, turn your palms out and lift your arms up in front, leading with your elbows. Then, lifting the thighs up toward the ceiling, start to plié.

B Carry on down into a deep plié, keeping the heels on the floor for as long as possible. Pull the energy up through the thighs, letting the heels come off the floor when they are ready. Go as deep as you can without losing the contraction.

SP   A

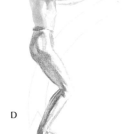

D

C Start the release at the pelvis, straightening the spine in sequence. Change your arms by dropping the elbows down and turning your palms to the front, pressing down through the whole of your back, especially the shoulder blades. Don't lean forward and don't sit on your heels. This will be the most difficult position to balance in.

D Continue lifting up through the torso, pushing your heels to the floor, so that you come through the demi-plié again but in a release. The arms push down, as if pushing down on a table top.

B

C

Parallel Pliés with Relevé

Your body alignment, posture and sense of centre can be worked on in many different ways. Don't close your mind to a way of working just because it "feels wrong", for our feelings of what seems right are often mistaken. People who stand with the pelvis slumped under, the chest caved in and the head jutting forward don't stand that way because they want to look like that, but because it feels right to them – they feel they are standing straight. If a teacher were to realign such a body manually to correct the posture they would undoubtedly say that it felt wrong. Feelings are not to be trusted. That is why dancers use mirrors in their training – so that they can see what their bodies are doing and rectify their mistakes.

The Sequence Start in parallel (SP) then, using a count of eight, do a small demi-plié (A), return to SP, go up to a relevé (B), return to SP, plié again (A), go straight up to the relevé (B), back to plié (A), return to SP and begin again. Do the exercise eight times, in two sets of four, taking a short rest after the first four. Tempo: slow.

SP. A SP B SP A B A SP x 8

Experiment with the sensation of body alignment by trying the exercise in two different ways. First, think of yourself as a tall tree rooted to the ground through your feet and do the entire sequence with an enormous feeling of strength and stability. Second, imagine your body to be a hollow cylinder through which water rushes up as you lower yourself (A, or returning to SP from B) and down as you rise up (B, or returning to SP from A).

SP Stand in 1st position parallel, with your arms by your sides. Keep your weight dead in the centre of your hip sockets and feet – don't lean forward on to the toes.

A Bend your knees into a small demi plié.

B Go up on to your half toes in a relevé.

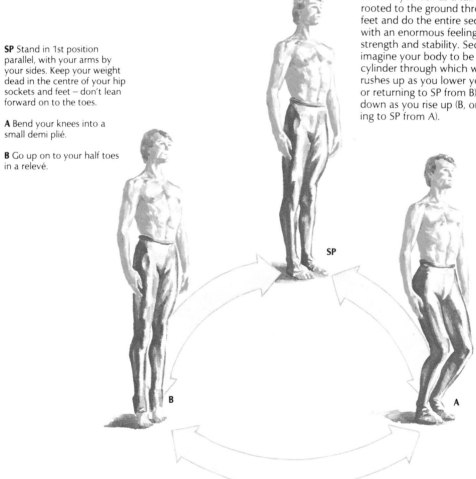

Turned Out Deep Pliés

Most people lack smooth coordination in their movements. So when we see someone move whose body works in harmony with itself and with the environment, we say that he or she has grace. A graceful body has a magical quality. It moves from within itself with an utter simplicity of function.

In today's world, we are constantly assaulted by a changing environment. Our way of coping with these assaults shows in how we walk or stand or move between positions. To regain a measure of grace we must teach our body parts to trust one another and train ourselves to move with harmony and a sense of personal direction. These deep pliés not only exercise the back and legs but also teach us to synchronize the movement of arms and legs.

Sequence 1 (Pliés in 1st) The sequence is in eight sets of three counts. From SP, demi-plié (A) 1, 2, 3; 2, 2, 3; go down to a deep plié (B) 3, 2, 3; 4, 2, 3; come up to a demi-plié, arms out to 2nd (C) 5, 2, 3; 6, 2, 3; then return to SP, 7, 2, 3; 8, 2, 3. Repeat the sequence three times, then point the right leg to 2nd (T) for two counts of three, put the right heel down and centre your weight for two counts of three, ready to do the exercise in 2nd (see p.132). Tempo: fast.

SP. A B C SP x 4. **T**

T (transition) Point the right leg to 2nd position, raising your left arm out to the side in opposition.

SP Stand with the legs turned out in 1st position, arms held in a long shallow curve by your sides.

A Demi-plié, pulling the thighs up and lifting your arms up in a long arc in front of you. Keep your heels on the floor and your arches raised.

B Carry on down into a deep plié, allowing the heels to lift up a little way off the floor, and continue the upward arc of the arms until they are above your head.

C Return to demi-plié, opening your arms out to 2nd position, palms up.

Sequence 2 (Pliés in 2nd) The only difference between doing the sequence in 1st position and in 2nd position is that in 2nd the heels remain on the floor and the arches stay up throughout the exercise. As you lift up your arms in positions A and B, pull down with your shoulder blades and rotate the upper arms in the shoulder joints. Don't lift your shoulders or collar bone. In the plié (B), go as deep as you can but take care not to lose your turn out or stick your pelvis out behind you. As before, the sequence takes eight sets of three counts and is repeated three times. Tempo: fast.

SP. A B C SP x 4

SP Stand with your legs turned out in 2nd position, arms curved in to your sides.

A Bend your knees in a demi-plié, lifting the arms up in front of you in a long half-oval curve. If you turn out the legs sufficiently, your knees will align with your middle toes and your arches will be high, like bridges under the feet.

SP

C

A

C Come halfway up again to a demi-plié, opening your arms out to 2nd position, palms up.

B

B Continue deepening the plié and lifting the arms up above your head. Your knees should extend beyond your toes this time. If they don't, your feet must be too wide apart.

Adagio

The slow, controlled movements of the adagio give you a chance to work on tuning your entire body. Each muscle has an enormous range of movement, from total relaxation to maximum contraction, and although you will hardly ever be at either end of that range while dancing, you will constantly be monitoring and controlling the subtle gradations of tension in your muscles as you move. Over a period of time, you should be able to gain awareness of the way the large groups of muscles move in relation to one another, and it is with this awareness that you should practise the adagio. The most difficult part of the exercise will be to keep the turn out of the standing leg – you will have to hold it from the hip socket down through the thigh and into the foot.

Sequence 1 Take four threes to plié (SP, A, B) and four to rise (C); eight threes to trace an arc with your right foot and slide back to 4th (D, E, F), and eight to balance in arabesque and finish in 1st (G, H, I). Repeat on the other side. Tempo: slow.

SP A B C D E F G H I x 2 (1 each side)

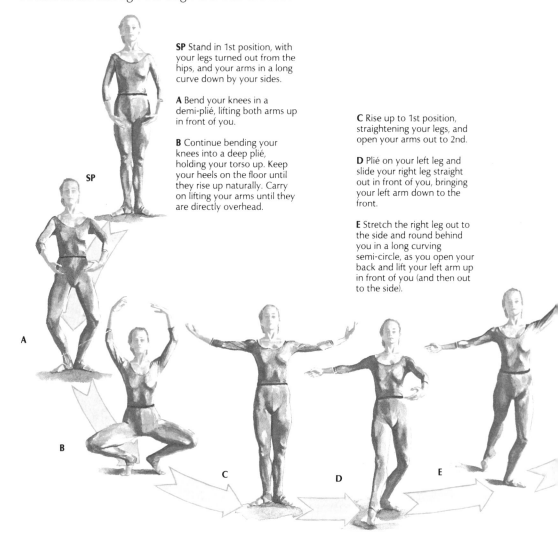

SP Stand in 1st position, with your legs turned out from the hips, and your arms in a long curve down by your sides.

A Bend your knees in a demi-plié, lifting both arms up in front of you.

B Continue bending your knees into a deep plié, holding your torso up. Keep your heels on the floor until they rise up naturally. Carry on lifting your arms until they are directly overhead.

C Rise up to 1st position, straightening your legs, and open your arms out to 2nd.

D Plié on your left leg and slide your right leg straight out in front of you, bringing your left arm down to the front.

E Stretch the right leg out to the side and round behind you in a long curving semi-circle, as you open your back and lift your left arm up in front of you (and then out to the side).

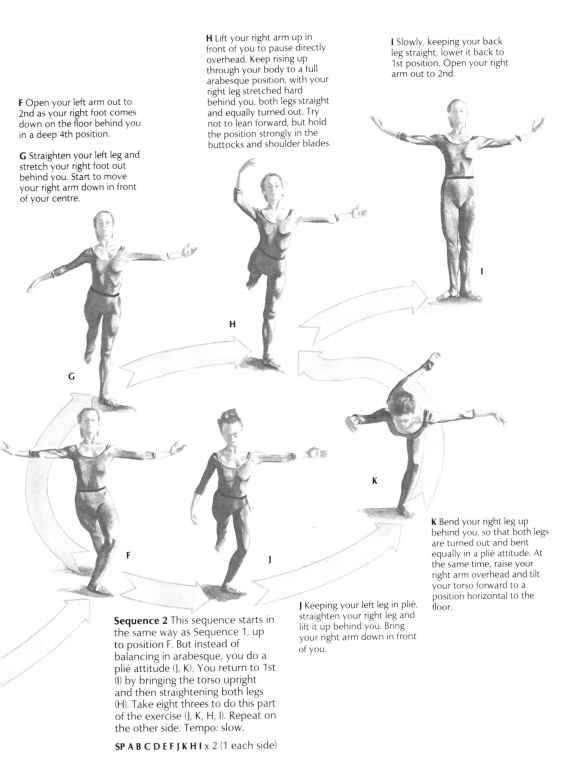

H Lift your right arm up in front of you to pause directly overhead. Keep rising up through your body to a full arabesque position, with your right leg stretched hard behind you, both legs straight and equally turned out. Try not to lean forward, but hold the position strongly in the buttocks and shoulder blades.

I Slowly, keeping your back leg straight, lower it back to 1st position. Open your right arm out to 2nd.

F Open your left arm out to 2nd as your right foot comes down on the floor behind you in a deep 4th position.

G Straighten your left leg and stretch your right foot out behind you. Start to move your right arm down in front of your centre.

K Bend your right leg up behind you, so that both legs are turned out and bent equally in a plié attitude. At the same time, raise your right arm overhead and tilt your torso forward to a position horizontal to the floor.

J Keeping your left leg in plié, straighten your right leg and lift it up behind you. Bring your right arm down in front of you.

Sequence 2 This sequence starts in the same way as Sequence 1, up to position F. But instead of balancing in arabesque, you do a plié attitude (J, K). You return to 1st (I) by bringing the torso upright and then straightening both legs (H). Take eight threes to do this part of the exercise (J, K, H, I). Repeat on the other side. Tempo: slow.

SP A B C D E F J K H I x 2 (1 each side)

Shifting Body Weight

When you did this exercise in the Basic section (p.84), you kept your back leg low to the floor. In the development of Shifting Body Weight, you are going to lift the back leg high into the air in the forward movement, and up into a plié attitude on the return, while doing a plié on the standing leg. In this part of the exercise, both legs are in relatively the same position, except that the standing leg will have your weight on it. It is important that you work them together and try to feel their relationship to each other.

The Sequence In five counts of three, starting at SP, step forward on to your left leg (A), step forward on to your right (B), step back on to your left again (C), plié in attitude (D) and return to SP. As you return to SP from D, lift your torso up first, then straighten both legs and step back on to your right leg. Repeat three times, finishing in plié attitude. Then do the exercise on the other side. Tempo: medium.

SP. A B C D SP x 3. **A B C D** (right leg)
SP. A B C D SP x 3. **A B C D** (left leg)

A Shift your weight forward on to your left leg. At the same time, lift the right leg to as high a 2nd position as you can hold. Bring your right arm out to 2nd and raise your left arm out to the side and up overhead, coordinating the movements with your leg.

B Step forward on to your right leg, holding the turn out. Keep your weight high in the torso, stretching the left foot hard behind you. Bring your left arm forward in basic opposition.

SP Stand with your weight on your right leg and the left leg stretched out in front of you. Keep both legs turned out, and hold your arms in opposition.

C Push back from the right leg and shift your weight back on to your left leg. Pass your right leg close to your left in the passé position, and raise both arms up in front of you, holding them in a long curve above your head. Keep your weight lifted high in the left thigh and hip socket.

D Still standing on the left leg, bring the right leg up behind you as high as you can in the attitude position. Plié on the left leg, increasing your turn out, and open your arms to 2nd. Hold your weight deep in the pelvis.

Body Arcs

Body arcs, or stretches to the sides of the body, exercise the torso in a different way from any of the methods you have tried so far. They are based on the deep, stretching curve you can make to the centre line that runs from your heels to the top of your head. You will find that the more you can push your weight into the floor and the more you are able to make the curve of the body even, the further you will be able to lean before falling off-balance.

As you work through the exercise, imagine that you are a tall tree, bending in the wind, with long roots tapering down from the soles of your feet into the ground. Practise swaying from side to side first until the movement is smooth and complete, using your entire body, legs and arms equally as you change sides. Take the exercise very slowly to begin with, as there is a great deal of internal movement to learn and coordinate. Later you can increase the tempo, as you become more familiar with the sequence.

The Sequence Take six single counts for this exercise, one for each time you lean. Starting at SP, lean to the right (A) 1, lean to the left (B) 2, lean to the right and lunge out to the side (C) 3, recover and lean to the left (B) 4, lean to the right and slide your right leg back (D) 5, recover and lean to the left (B) 6, then start the whole sequence again by leaning to the right (A). Repeat the exercise three times, rest, then repeat on the left side. Tempo: very slow.

SP. A B C B D B x 4 (right side) SP. A B C B D B x 4 (left side) SP

SP Stand in 1st position, legs turned out and arms held in a long, shallow curve.

A Keeping your feet firmly planted on the floor, lean over to the right, pushing your right hip out to the side. Pull up high in the torso and arch your spine so that you are also leaning backward slightly. Curve your right arm out to the side and hold your left arm in a long shallow curve to counterbalance the lean to the right.

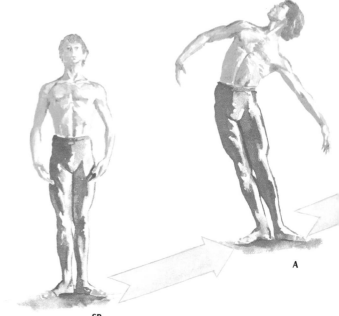

SP

A

C As you lean over to the right, allow your weight to fall back and be caught by your left leg in a lunge.

B Lean over to the left, mirroring the movements described for position A.

D As you lean over to the right, pulling up high in the torso, lean back too, arching the spine until you start to fall backward. Quickly break the legs apart by sliding the right leg back, keeping the knee straight, and plié on the standing leg.

Contraction in 2nd

The basic exercise (p.86) deals only with the contraction and its release. Here you will be developing the release part of the movement, using the energy not only to release the back and turn out, but also to move the right leg in a long, generous arc. Be careful on the release to keep the standing leg turned out and the torso lifted high so that the other leg is free to swing in a circle without tilting the pelvis. You will need to develop a strong internal pressure to repeat the same circular movement with the leg.

The Sequence Take eight threes to complete this exercise: two threes to contract (SP to A); two to release and swing the leg round in an arc (B, C, D); two to swing the leg round again (E, F, G, H); two to contract (I) and two to release back to SP. Do the exercise twice on each side, then rest and repeat again. Tempo: medium.

SP. A B C D E F G H I SP x 4 (2 each side)

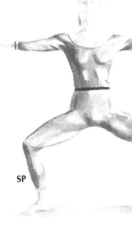

SP Start in 2nd position, legs in demi-plié and arms outstretched, palms facing upward.

F Raise your left arm overhead, keeping your right arm stretched out to the side. Lift your right leg up in front of you, pointing the foot.

G Open both arms out to the sides as your right leg moves out to 2nd (as in C).

H Bring your right arm down and up in a three-quarter circle as you swing your right leg behind you in another 4th position lunge.

I Move into another contraction by tilting your pelvis (as in A). Swing the right side of your body around to the left in a parallel position, passing your right leg close to your left. Return to SP by releasing your spine and pulling your right leg back through 4th and out to 2nd, keeping the same plié. Lift your arms up overhead and then out to the sides.

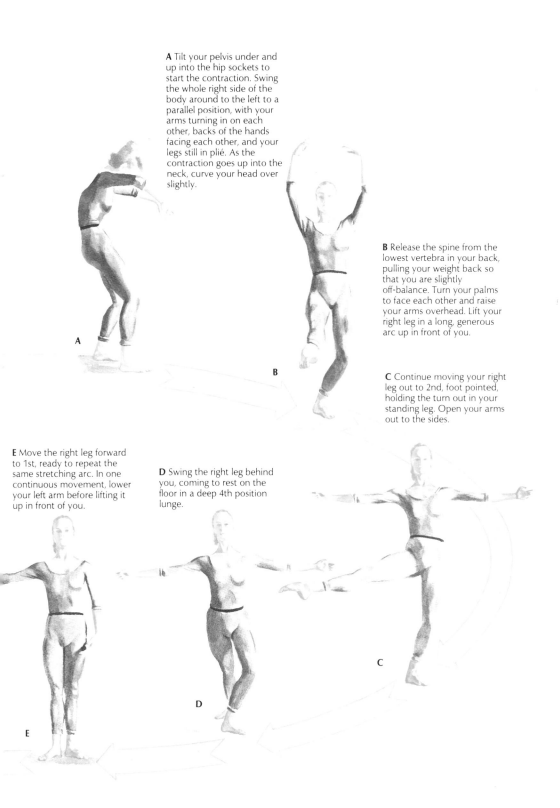

A Tilt your pelvis under and up into the hip sockets to start the contraction. Swing the whole right side of the body around to the left to a parallel position, with your arms turning in on each other, backs of the hands facing each other, and your legs still in plié. As the contraction goes up into the neck, curve your head over slightly.

B Release the spine from the lowest vertebra in your back, pulling your weight back so that you are slightly off-balance. Turn your palms to face each other and raise your arms overhead. Lift your right leg in a long, generous arc up in front of you.

C Continue moving your right leg out to 2nd, foot pointed, holding the turn out in your standing leg. Open your arms out to the sides.

E Move the right leg forward to 1st, ready to repeat the same stretching arc. In one continuous movement, lower your left arm before lifting it up in front of you.

D Swing the right leg behind you, coming to rest on the floor in a deep 4th position lunge.

Jumps

In order to help yourself jump, think of your body as a compressed spring which, when released, will spring directly up into the air. But don't compress your body so much that you constrain your muscles – you should tighten the muscles purely to gain the proper strength and tension necessary for the jump. When you finally develop the strength in your legs and back to jump repeatedly straight up in the air, you will experience a wonderful feeling of control. Repeated jumps are also a marvellous way of gaining endurance and a sense of breath, and of developing your speed of reaction, and this will reflect through all the rest of your work.

Jumps in 5th

Although jumps in 5th are quite simple movements, they are extremely difficult to do well and are most demanding on your sense of centre. You should be able to jump up and down on the same spot, keeping a sense of balance, so that you don't start swinging or rotating in the air.

The Sequence As a prelude to the sequence, try doing the jumps one at a time. Starting in SP, plié (A), jump up (B), change legs (C), land in plié (D), straighten your legs (SP) and stop. Repeat on the other side. Once you are familiar with the sensation of jumping and landing, you can try the sequence itself, doing four jumps at a time in four counts (punctuating each count with "and"). Start the counting on the "and" as you jump into the air, landing on the "one" count, jumping and changing legs on the "and", and so on (and 1 and 2 and 3 and 4). Do this four times. Tempo: medium.

SP. A B C D C B A B C D C B A SP x 4

As your endurance builds up, try doing eight jumps, then 16, and finally 32, all without stopping while still maintaining your body alignment and centre.

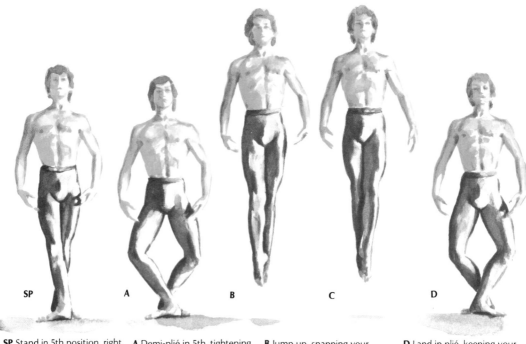

SP Stand in 5th position, right leg in front, right heel to left big toe, and hips and legs turned out. Hold your arms down by your sides.

A Demi-plié in 5th, tightening the buttocks and backs of the thighs so that your weight doesn't fall forward.

B Jump up, snapping your feet up off the floor.

C Change legs in mid-air, opening them slightly, to left leg front, right leg back.

D Land in plié, keeping your back straight and the arches of your feet up.

Jumps in 1st, 2nd and 4th

A dancer needs enormous stamina to jump up and down many times. Jumping exercises such as these will strengthen the body and so help to avoid injury. When you have built up sufficient confidence, you can make up your own combinations of jumps. Make sure you know how many sets you are going to do before starting, and be careful to keep the rhythm steady at a tempo you can maintain.

The Sequence As with Jumps in 5th (p.142), you will land on the beat, and jump up on the "and". Starting at SP, demi-plié (B), jump up in 1st (A), land in 1st (B), jump up in 1st with arms up (C), land in 2nd (D), jump up in 2nd (E), land in 4th, right leg front (F), jump up in 4th (G), land in 4th, left leg front (H), then jump up in 1st (A), and do the whole sequence again. Do the exercise four times (making four sets of four counts) finishing with one extra jump so that you end in 1st. Rest and then do four more sets, bringing the left leg in 4th position to the front first. Tempo: medium.

SP B. A B C D E F G H x 4. **A B SP**

SP   A   B   C

SP Stand in 1st position, both legs turned out, arms by your sides.

A Jump straight up, making your feet snap up off the floor.

B Land in 1st position demi-plié, heels just touching each other.

C Jump up in 1st, lifting both arms up in front of you.

D Land in 2nd position demi-plié. As you come down, open your arms out to the sides.

D   E   F   G   H

E Jump up, your arms and legs stretched out in 2nd.

F Land in 4th position demi-plié, right leg front. Bring your left arm forward in opposition as you descend.

G Jump up in 4th, changing legs in mid-air, to left leg front. Open your left arm back out to 2nd.

H Land in 4th position demi-plié, left leg front. Bring your right arm forward in opposition as you descend.

MOVING IN SPACE: Side Triplets

The basic triplet (p.94) can be used in many different ways. You can do it sideways, backwards, turning around and from side to side, as in the following combination. Although it is a good exercise to do on its own because of its rhythm and stretching movements, it is also used as a transition sequence to link other steps or positions together. When using these side triplets as part of a dance movement, do them with as much internal stretch and resonance as you can feel. The tempo can be fast or slow, as long as the whole movement is smooth, long and sensuous.

The Sequence On a count of three, starting with the right leg back (SP), lunge to the left (A) 1; rise up and lean to the right (B), stretch and point your right foot (C) 2; fall back on to your right leg (B) 3; then lunge over to the right (A – right side) and do the sequence on the other side. Repeat for eight threes, then do the exercise again starting with the left leg back. Tempo: medium.

SP (right leg back) **A** (left) **B C B A** (right) **B C B** x 4
SP (left leg back) **A** (right) **B C B A** (left) **B C B** x 4

SP Stand with your left leg turned out and your right leg stretched behind you, your right foot in relevé. Stretch the whole right side of your body up, your right arm held high, so that you lean over to the left. Hold your left arm out to the side as a counterbalance.

C Take your weight back on to your left leg on the half-toe and momentarily stretch and point your right leg in front.

B Move your weight to your right leg until you can rise up on it. Change the stretch in your body to your left side, stretching your left leg behind on the half-toe and your left arm up to the ceiling. Hold your right arm out to the side.

A Lunge out to 2nd position plié, stretching your torso even further to your left. Hold both arms out to the left in a long curving arc.

The Leap

Before you experiment with different leaps, you should practise the basic leap (p.97) with both legs as straight as possible. This is the most classic leap of all, even if its clean, simple lines make it the most difficult. Three variations on the basic leap are shown here, although there are many more, especially in contemporary dance. Remember that in order to leap successfully, you need to coordinate the change of arms and legs, the push off the back leg forward and into the front leg, and the lift of the torso up into space. Don't try to leap too high at first – just get a feeling for the rhythm involved. Height will come into your leap with practice.

Front Leg Bent Sometimes called a "stag" leap, you can practise this leap in the leap preparations (p.97) by bringing the leg up in a high bent-kneed position instead of swinging it up straight. Keep the lower leg tucked under as you leap and try to raise the torso on the lifted thigh as if you were making a high step up into the air. Hold the back leg very strongly from the buttocks down to support the muscles of the back.

Be careful on landing as you can go higher on this leap than you might expect. The bent front leg should not turn out, but the back leg should be fully open.

Front Leg Bent

Back Leg Bent Rather like an athlete clearing a hurdle, you should keep your front leg straight and your back leg bent in an attitude position. Try to get a long, high stretch between the legs.

Back Leg Bent

Curved Leap

Curved Leap In this leap, the back is curved over and both legs are bent with the front leg turned out. It relates closely to the hip spiral contraction position (p.116). As you leap, the contraction curve of the spine should be timed to help take you up into the air with an up-and-over feeling – rather like a horse taking a fence. If you curve your spine too early, the contraction will throw you down. You should release the spine easily on landing to help cushion your weight through your leg. Be careful on landing that you are not leaning too far forward and that your front leg is strong.

Development Workout Chart

The Development Workout Chart includes exercises from both the basic and development sessions. In order for you to learn how to integrate the development exercises in your workout, I have grouped all the Floorwork, Centrework and Moving in Space exercises together, so that the basic version of an exercise (marked B on the chart) is immediately followed by its development form (D). Thus, you will see under Floorwork, Contractions (B) followed by Contractions (D). (Note that not all basic exercises have development forms, and vice versa.)

FLOORWORK		SHORT	REGULAR A	REGULAR B
Sitting spine stretches	B	●	●	●
Breathing	B	●	●	●
Contractions	B			
Contractions	D	●	●	●
Leg exercises	B			
Leg exercises	D		●	
Arm exercises	B			
Side stretches	B		●	
Heel in hand stretches	D		(Seq 1) ●	(Seq 2) ●
Parallel leg flexes	B			
Combination flex and point	D			●
Hip spiral	D		●	●
Side falls	D		●	
Leg lifts and spine stretches	D		●	●
Contraction arches	D			●
Kneeling spine curls	B			
Kneeling spine curls	D	●		
Rising from the floor	B			
Rising from the floor	D	●	●	●

CENTREWORK	
Use of parallel and turn out	B
Parallel and turn out	D
Parallel leg beats	B
Parallel pliés	B
Parallel contractions	B
Parallel pliés with contractions	D
Parallel pliés with relevé	D
Turned out leg beats	B
Turned out demi-pliés	B
Turned out demi-pliés/breath	B
Turned out deep pliés/arms	D
Adagio	D
Shifting body weight	B
Shifting body weight	D
Body arcs	D
Contraction in 2nd	B
Contraction in 2nd	D
Jump preparations	B
Jumps in 1st and 2nd	B
Jumps in 5th	D
Jumps in 1st, 2nd and 4th	D

I have provided you with three development workouts – a short one, which you should tackle first, or use if you are pushed for time, and two "regular" ones, A and B. Learn the development exercises listed in the short workout first, and include them in your basic workout, adding one every three sessions. Then start learning the remaining ones on the chart. Don't push yourself too quickly – remember that it is much more important to do an exercise well than to learn a lot of exercises and do them only half-well. As you progress through the development exercises, it becomes more vital than ever to work consistently and not miss sessions.

Once you have learned all the development exercises, alternate between Regular Workout A and B. If you get bored of repeating the exercises every day or feel that you have reached a plateau and are no longer progressing, don't worry – it's quite natural. This plateau is one that every dancer has to work through in order to improve. After long periods where nothing seems to be happening you will find that suddenly you make a breakthrough and everything changes.

	ORT	REGULAR A	REGULAR B
•		•	•
•		•	
•			•
•		•	
•			
•			•
		•	
		•	
			•
			•
•		•	•
		•	
		•	
			•
•		•	•
•		•	•
		•	
•			•

MOVING IN SPACE		SHORT	REGULAR A	REGULAR B
Walking	B			
Walk with balance	B		•	
Low walk	B			•
Triplet	B		•	
Side triplets	D		•	•
Skip	B	•		•
Leap	B		•	
Leap	D			•

Development Dance Sequences

By now you should know enough dance movement to make up your own dance sequences. Ideally you should be combining floorwork or centrework exercises with travelling steps so that the entire sequence moves in space. As in the Basic Dance Sequences (pp.102-5), you should try to keep the tempo consistent, using multiples of the same rhythm to count the sequence. For instance, if you started on a fast tempo of two beats per second, you could either take one running step per beat, or one walking step every fourth beat. Of course there are no hard and fast rules – you can always change the tempo completely within any sequence, but it is very difficult to do and will require careful attention.

When devising your own sequence, you should also bear in mind the overall shape your sequence makes in space, and ensure that the transitions between exercises are done smoothly and with control.

The Combination To summarize, this sequence involves four Triplets (p.94), three Side Triplets (p.145), a balance in arabesque, a Side Fall (pp.118-20), four more Triplets (p.94), and five Leaps (pp.97, 146).

Start in the upper left-hand corner of your space. On a count of three, do four triplets diagonally across the room toward the lower right-hand corner, leading off with your right leg. On the last step of the fourth triplet, plié instead of relevé, turn round to face the centre and step on to your right leg in 2nd position plié. You will now be in a position to do three side triplets in three threes: first to the right, then left, then right again. As you step on to your left leg to begin the fourth three, turn to face your left side, plié and straighten up in arabesque (to finish the fourth three).

Now swing your arms in a full circle on three counts, and in three more threes, side fall to the floor and rise again to arabesque on the left leg. Curving to the left, do four triplets in a large semi-circle, returning to your original starting

position. Use the fourth triplet as a preparation for a leap on to your right leg, so that you land on the "one" count of the next three. Do four leaps diagonally across your space, varying each leap. In the first leap, both legs should be straight; in the second, your front leg should be straight and your back leg bent; in the third, bend your front leg and keep your back leg straight, and in the fourth, both legs should be bent.

The whole combination should take you 20 threes to complete. Good luck.

Jazz Dance

Jazz dance is fun. But it is not just a free-form style where you dance around doing your own thing. It has its own rules, just like ballet, and requires you to have a very free and flexible body, together with the ability to "isolate" all its separate parts. This ability will help you to keep to the rhythm of the music almost as if your body were another jazz instrument – hitting the beats with a hip movement, a quick leg beat or a shoulder move. Indeed, some movements are so fast and intricate, that they seem to pick up and reflect the multiple rhythms of jazz music in much the same way as the facets of a cut stone reflect light.

What makes jazz dance so different from other kinds of dance? Its look is unmistakable, yet its style can vary greatly, absorbing the many influences of current life and fashions. It can be clean and cool, abstract and slightly remote; or it can be lusty, sensuous and very energetic. Jazz dance is often associated with musicals, where it can be used to express contemporary urban themes as in Jerome Robbins' *West Side Story*. But whatever the style, whether fast or lyrical, there is no doubt that it is a highly skilled and very powerful form of dance.

Jazz dance has always been more popular in the States than in Europe, but that is not surprising when you delve into its history. It probably started among the black dancers in the southern United States, and grew out of a combination of tap dance and early American show dancing. But the two people who I regard as being the most influential in developing the kind of dance we now recognize as Jazz are Katherine Dunham and Jack Cole.

Katherine Dunham, brilliant performer and anthropologist, was fascinated by the dances of the Caribbean. Having conducted her own researches into them, she devised her own teaching methods and went on to dance on Broadway. She then formed her own dance company and choreographed a huge number of spectacular dances, performing all over the United States and Europe during the 1940s and '50s. Her dances were based on Afro-Caribbean movements, but produced as American stage shows. She had great theatrical flair, and her dancers were exciting and appealing. Her school in New York attracted many young dancers, and there was a time in the 1950s when everyone seemed to be practising pelvic and spine isolations. She also trained many teachers and her techniques and ideas have now become embodied in almost every jazz class.

The other major influence was Jack Cole. He was a member of the Ted Shawn all-male dance company in the late 1930s, and so came from the same background as other modern dance innovators such as Martha Graham and Doris Humphrey. His main contribution to jazz dance was to make an unlikely marriage between classic Indian dance and American jazz music. He also studied Brazilian dance and Cuban rumba, and out of this strange mixture evolved the dance form in the 1940s and '50s that was known as jazz dance. An electric performer himself, Jack Cole choreographed many Broadway musicals, and is said to have taught Marilyn Monroe everything she knew about dance.

Jazz dance is a very personal and creative form of dance, as once you have learned the technique, you can give way to your own spontaneity. You can jazz dance to whatever music is currently popular – the livelier, the better. And all the while you are having fun, you are strengthening your body, increasing your speed and improving your coordination.

Body Rolls

Before a rehearsal or even a class, dancers usually do a warm up, repeating a few simple sequences. Body rolls are one of the best ways of warming up, for they involve the entire body in a sequential roll. You should feel that you are stretching as much as is possible within your body frame, rather like a cat stretches itself after lying down, before moving off. The exercise will also help you to focus your attention inside yourself, increasing your body awareness, especially if you try it with your eyes closed.

The Sequence Take six counts to stretch up from SP through A and B to C, and six to return back to SP (via D and E), doing the "break" (D) on the "one" count. Repeat three times, then rest and repeat again. Tempo: slow.

SP. A B C D E SP x 4

With experience you should aim to do the whole sequence on two sets of four counts, and finally on two sets of two.

E Continue the controlled collapse by rolling your hips under, curving the spine up and dropping your head forward.

SP Start in a parallel position, each foot directly under its own hip socket. Drop the body forward, curving the spine from the base to the head.

A Start pulling back and down at the base of the spine and up against the front of the abdomen to rise up in sequence through the spine. Begin to straighten the knees.

B Rise to vertical, keeping your back long and straight. Let your arms bend up at the elbows.

C Continue the direction of the lift up through the arms extending them straight up and stretching out through the fingertips. Turn your palms to the front.

D Break the upward stretch by opening and bending the joints of the knees, hips, neck, elbows and wrists all at the same time. There will be a slight arching of the back. Turn your palms toward you.

Tendues with Pliés

Tendues with pliés are a combination of two exercises that you have already done – Leg Beats or tendues (p.76) and Parallel Pliés (p.77). They are performed, however, with a different timing and feeling in the body, and have a certain neatness which makes them valuable not only for technical training, but also for body attitudes. Besides working your stretching leg to the front, you are also going to work it to the side and back (p.158). The plié positions are particularly characteristic of jazz dance, with the bend of the knees closely related to the bend of the elbows.

SP Start in a closed parallel position, arms by your sides.

A Stretch your right leg out in front, pointing the toes.

B With a sudden but lifted movement, drop into a plié, opening your arms out to the sides. Pull back slightly in your right hip socket so that you can elongate and stretch the inside of your right leg. Don't lift your arms too high and try to relate the bend of your elbows to the bend of your knees.

C Straighten up, stretching your right leg out in front.

The Sequence From a closed parallel position (SP), you are going to extend your right leg forward (A), drop suddenly into a demi-plié (B), straighten up (C), and then close back to parallel (SP). Now, continuing on page 158, repeat the same pattern, but this time point your right leg out to 2nd (SP, D, E, F, SP). You will find it hard at first to keep parallel in this position, but if you study yourself in the mirror, you should be able to make your legs look right as well as feel right. Then do the whole movement pointing your right leg to the back (SP, G, H, I, SP). Do the whole sequence to the right on three sets of four counts, and then repeat on the left side. Tempo: slow.

SP. A B C SP D E F SP G H I SP x 2 (both sides)

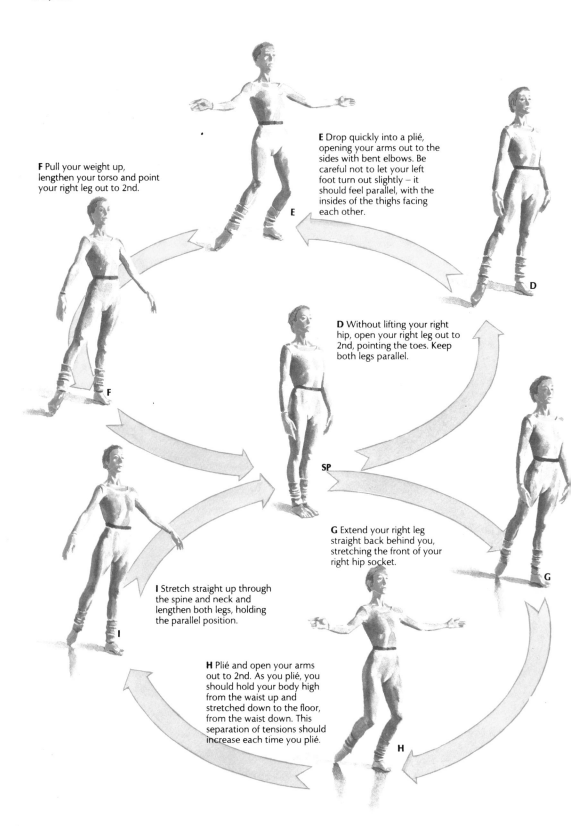

E Drop quickly into a plié, opening your arms out to the sides with bent elbows. Be careful not to let your left foot turn out slightly – it should feel parallel, with the insides of the thighs facing each other.

F Pull your weight up, lengthen your torso and point your right leg out to 2nd.

D Without lifting your right hip, open your right leg out to 2nd, pointing the toes. Keep both legs parallel.

G Extend your right leg straight back behind you, stretching the front of your right hip socket.

I Stretch straight up through the spine and neck and lengthen both legs, holding the parallel position.

H Plié and open your arms out to 2nd. As you plié, you should hold your body high from the waist up and stretched down to the floor, from the waist down. This separation of tensions should increase each time you plié.

Flex and Point

A good jazz sequence improves not only your legs and sense of balance, but also your coordination. Since you will be doing several different things at once, this exercise will take some time to perfect. It is best learned by a process of accumulation, like learning lines by heart. Try to work out the sensations in each moving part individually, and then combine the sensations together as you build up confidence. Basically, you will be flexing and pointing your leg first to the front, then to the side, and finally behind you, while changing your arm positions. During all these leg lifts, you should take care not to compensate by leaning your torso in the opposite direction to which your leg is raised, and don't lift the hip on the extending leg.

SP Stand in 1st position parallel, arms by your sides. Hold this position strongly.

A Lift your arms up, right arm out to the side, left arm bent in, level with your chest. Extend your right leg out in front of you and flex the foot.

B Reverse the position of your arms so that the right arm is bent in and the left arm is extended out to 2nd. At the same time, point your right foot, keeping your weight high on your standing leg.

C Holding your shoulder blades strongly, extend your left arm out to the side, so that both arms are stretched out and away from you. Point your right foot.

D Lower your right leg to the floor, keeping the foot pointed and strong. As your leg goes down, pull up and back in the body to give you strength for the next movement.

The Sequence Taking one count for each movement, the whole sequence can be done in six sets of eight counts. Starting from a parallel position (SP), stretch your right leg forward and flex (A), point (B), flex (A), point (B), flex (A) again, then point your foot and open your arms (C). Lower your foot to the floor (D) and close to SP by resisting the urge to flatten your right foot.

The next part of the sequence repeats the same pattern, only you flex and point your right foot out to the side. Thus: flex (E) and point (F) twice, flex (E) again, point and open your arms (G), lower to the floor (H) and return to SP. *The sequence continues overleaf.*

E Keeping the standing leg parallel, turn and lift your right leg out to the side, foot flexed. Try to resist the tendency to lean your body over to the left in compensation. Lift both arms, bending your left arm in and extending your right arm out to the side.

F Reverse your arms as you point your right foot. Again, resist leaning to the left. Be careful not to lift your right hip or shorten the waist on the right side.

G Concentrating on the centre line that runs up through your body as a means of holding your balance, extend your left arm out to the side (so that both arms are extended) and point your right foot.

H Lower your right leg to the floor, pointing the foot.

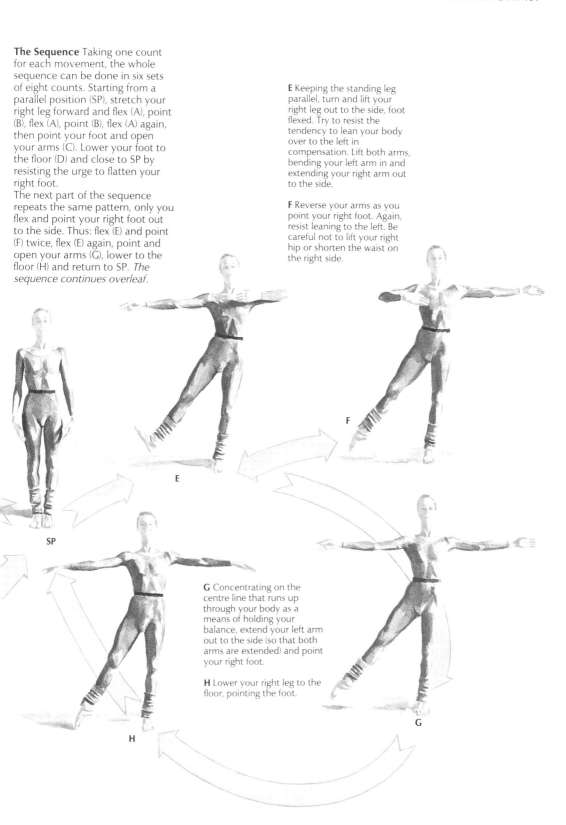

The Sequence (continued) From SP, repeat the pattern of flexing and pointing described on the previous pages, only with your right leg stretched behind you (I, J, I, J, I, K, L, SP). It will help if you keep your waist stretched up out of the pelvis, and your lower back long and open. Think of the process of lifting as a stretching and lengthening movement, not a shortening, cramping one. Once you have completed the exercise on the right side, repeat on the left (front, side and back), then do the whole exercise again. Tempo: slow.

SP. A B A B A C D SP E F E F E G H SP I J I J I K L SP x 4 (2 each side)

I Raise both arms, bending the left arm in and stretching the right out to the side. Extend your right leg back with the foot flexed. Be careful not to shorten your right leg.

J Change your arms as you point your right foot, lengthening the leg as you go from flex to point.

K Open your left arm out to the side as you point your right foot. Make sure you are holding yourself up using your back muscles.

L Lower your right leg to the floor, taking care not to jam your foot against the surface.

Jazz 4th

An unusual position but one that is very typical of jazz dance is this turned-in, side-facing 4th position. Depending on the strength in your legs and your ability to hold your weight up, you can actually "toe in" (turn your toes inward) with the feet. This exercise will also help you to learn the sensation of holding your weight very strongly in your thighs and pelvis while moving. In the plié, try to design the shape of your body so there is a sense of balance in the legs and arms. The pelvis has to relate strongly to the bent-under knee so that you can hold your weight up without straining your knees. Avoid starting in too wide a 2nd position, as your body will begin to fall down between your legs in the plié.

The Sequence The exercise is in eight counts: four to plié (SP, A, B, C) and four to return to SP (D, SP). As you slowly turn your body from D to SP, your left arm should describe a large circle overhead and finally open out to 2nd. Repeat on the other side, then do the whole exercise again. Tempo: very slow.

SP. A B C D SP x 4 (2 each side)

SP Stand in a strong wide 2nd position, with your arms held out to the sides at shoulder level, palms turned slightly down.

A Rotate your left hip toward your right, keeping your weight high in your waist. Hold your left leg straight, but let your left heel come up off the floor.

B As you continue turning your left hip to face your right side, your whole torso will turn as well, bringing your left arm in front of your torso and out to the right. Turn your left leg in by rotating on the ball of your foot. Keep your right arm out to the side.

C Plié on both legs as if you were going to kneel on your left knee. Keep your weight high in the torso.

D Return to standing by pulling straight up, then stretch the left side up, lifting your left arm overhead.

Jazz 4th Contraction

This exercise is another version of Jazz 4th. Once again, the movement is very typical of jazz dance, especially the deeply curved back. You will find it very useful in dance sequences as you can get into the plié position from many other positions, for instance from lunging forward on to the right leg or falling back on to your left leg, or you can use it to finish a turn or as part of a sequence rising up from the floor. Do practise the exercise carefully before using it in this way, however, as the position needs to be fully imprinted on the body's muscular memory to look right.

The Sequence Take eight counts for this exercise: four to go into the contraction plié (SP, A, B), and four to return to SP (C, SP). Lift the torso up high and bring both arms down by your sides as you turn your body back to 2nd. Repeat on the other side, and then do the whole exercise again. Tempo: very slow.

SP. A B C SP x 4 (2 each side)

SP Stand in a wide 2nd position with your arms down at your sides.

C Return to standing by releasing your spine and stretching up through the torso. Lift your left arm up overhead while still facing your right side.

A Contract under and up into your pelvis in order to rotate around your central axis to the right. Keeping your left leg straight at first, allow your left heel to come off the floor. As you turn the left side of your body around to the right in the contraction, resist the urge to turn back with your right side.

B Deepen your contraction, bending your knees into a plié. Bring your arms up using the back muscles, left arm stretched out in front of you, right arm out to the side.

Head Rolls

For its size, the head is the heaviest part of the body, acting as a counterbalance for any movement made elsewhere. Louis Horst, the great American dance teacher, used to say: "If you move your right little finger you should be able to feel it in your right earlobe." To move your head well, your neck needs to be flexible. But in most people, stress causes the muscles of the upper back and neck to tighten up. These head rolls are therefore very important, both to loosen and stretch the neck and to develop strength in the neck muscles. While doing the exercise, it may help if you imagine you have a little flag sticking up from the centre of your head, and you are waving it in ever-increasing circles.

The Sequence Starting at SP, in four counts, roll your head forward (A), right (B), back (C), left (D), then return to front (A) and repeat the sequence three times. Do the exercise four times in the reverse direction. Keep your spine long and stretched throughout. Tempo: medium.

SP. A B C D x 4 **SP. A D C B** x 4. **SP**

You can vary the exercise by only doing A to C and back to A, or B, D, B, D, etc.

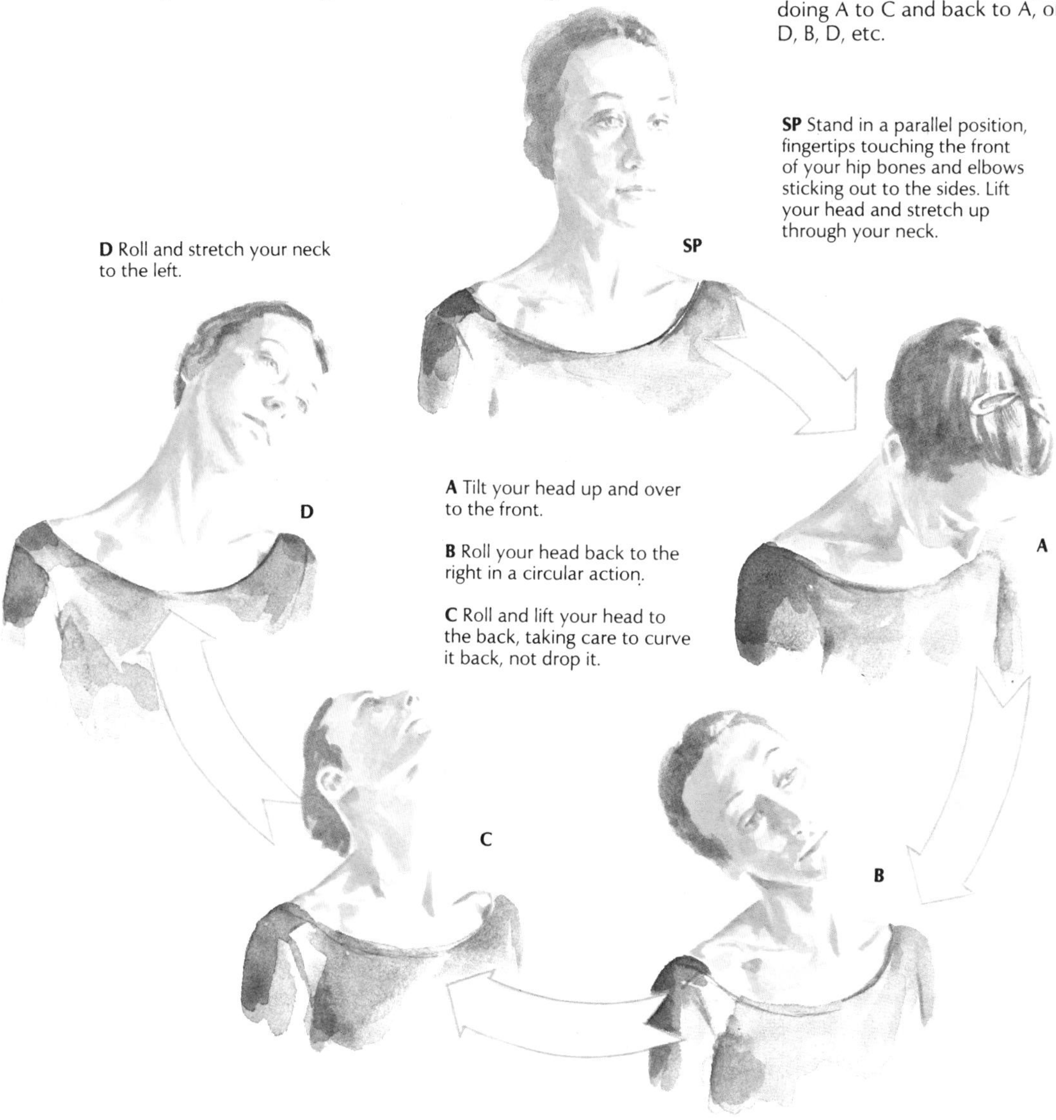

SP Stand in a parallel position, fingertips touching the front of your hip bones and elbows sticking out to the sides. Lift your head and stretch up through your neck.

D Roll and stretch your neck to the left.

SP

D

A Tilt your head up and over to the front.

B Roll your head back to the right in a circular action.

C Roll and lift your head to the back, taking care to curve it back, not drop it.

A

C

B

Shoulder Isolations

In jazz dance, you sometimes want to have a free-moving look to your body. All your joints must be able to move quickly in isolation so that you can hit one beat with a hip move, say, and the next with a shoulder move. Like the neck, the shoulders tend to stiffen up when you first begin to exercise them due to concentration and stress. Since your shoulders are extremely expressive parts of your body, you must become sensitive at all times to where they are in a position and how you are holding them. These shoulder isolations will not only increase your awareness of them, but also increase their flexibility, and will help you in all kinds of dance as well as jazz.

SP Stand in a parallel position, feet slightly apart. Hold your arms out to the sides, elbows bent, palms facing front. Bend your knees into a demi-plié and hold your weight strongly in the thighs and torso. Don't let any part of your body move except your shoulders.

SP

The Sequence This exercise can be done in two counts: one to lift your shoulders up, forward and down (SP, A, B), and two to return to SP (through A). Throughout the exercise, resist any temptation to pull the shoulders back, pinching the shoulder blades together. Repeat seven times. Tempo: medium.

SP. A B A SP x 8

Once you have mastered moving both shoulders together, try moving them one at a time, devising some new combinations.

A Lift your shoulders straight up.

A

B

B Roll your shoulders forward and down.

Shoulder Isolations with Contraction

Once you have perfected the simple shoulder isolations, you should try using your shoulders to motivate a contraction and lunge forward. This is a very strong movement, requiring you to throw your entire weight behind it. As a jazz dance movement, it can be used to punctuate a rhythm pattern or to begin or end a sequence. You can do it either very slowly, emphasizing all the parts of the movement, or very quickly, using a great deal of energy.

The Sequence Take four counts to do this exercise. Starting at SP, lift your shoulders (A) 1; contract and lunge forward (B) 2; release and lift your shoulders (C) 3; step back and rise up (SP) 4. Repeat four times on each side. Tempo: slow.

SP. A B C SP x 8 (4 each side)

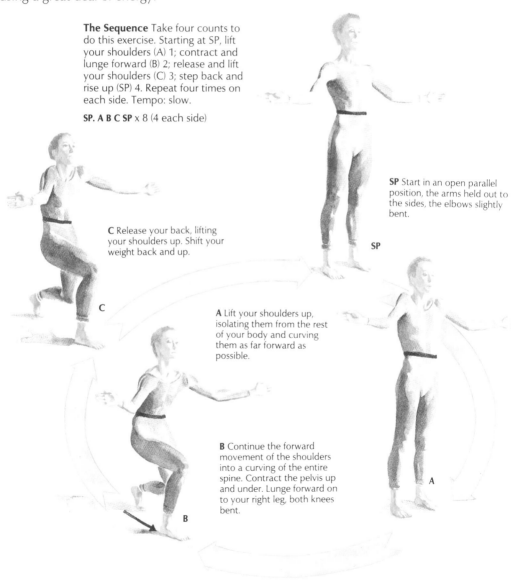

C Release your back, lifting your shoulders up. Shift your weight back and up.

SP Start in an open parallel position, the arms held out to the sides, the elbows slightly bent.

SP

A Lift your shoulders up, isolating them from the rest of your body and curving them as far forward as possible.

B Continue the forward movement of the shoulders into a curving of the entire spine. Contract the pelvis up and under. Lunge forward on to your right leg, both knees bent.

A

B

Rib Isolations

In the following exercise you will move your ribcage independently from the rest of your torso – first, from side to side, and then forward and back. The movement forward and back may be harder and more difficult to feel than the side-to-side movement. As you will discover, for jazz dance you need not only flexibility, but also as much control over all the parts of your body as possible. It will help you to learn these isolations if you think of your torso in terms of its separate parts.

Sequence 1 In this exercise you will move your ribs from side to side eight times in eight sets of two counts. Thus, starting in SP, move right (A), return to centre (SP), move left (B), return to centre (SP), and so on. Put your hand across the back of your waist and see if you can locate the movement in the spine. Concentrate on this place to achieve isolation of the ribcage. Rest and repeat. Tempo: medium.

SP. A SP B SP x 4

SP

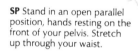

SP Stand in an open parallel position, hands resting on the front of your pelvis. Stretch up through your waist.

A Push straight across the ribcage to the right, at the level of the bottom of the breastbone. Be careful to go directly from side to side, not diagonally forward. Try not to move your pelvis.

B Repeat the same movement as in A, but to the left.

Sequence 2 Also in eight sets of two counts, move your ribs forward (C), return to centre (SP), move back (D), return to centre (SP), and so on. Rest and repeat. Tempo: medium.

SP. C SP D SP x 4

SP

C Lift your ribcage up and directly forward. Resist moving your pelvis forward. Hold your arms strong and back, but don't let the elbows point behind you.

D Move the ribcage straight back – do not simply depress the ribs. Try to move through the centre of the chest without moving your head and pelvis.

Hip Isolations

The pelvis plays a key role in jazz dance. It is used not only as a source of movement, as in any modern dance, but also to make rhythmical accents and gestures, like the head or arms. To move functionally and with grace, it is imperative that your pelvis is really sensitive to movement — for if you can't feel your pelvis, you lose the connection between your torso and your legs. Hip Isolations will allow you to rediscover your pelvis, if you have problems in maintaining contact with it. They will also help you to develop the kind of quick response to rhythm that is fundamental to jazz dance.

SP Start in an open parallel position, with your knees bent in a small demi-plié so that you feel strong in the thighs. Hold your arms out to the sides.

A Move your pelvis directly to the right, using the inner muscles of the thighs. Resist the tendency to lift the pelvis.

Sequence 1 In this isolation you are going to move the pelvis from right to left. As you move, try to "open" your waist and hip sockets, so that your pelvis is free to move but still strong. The sequence is in eight sets of two counts. Starting at SP, move to the right (A), return to centre (SP), move to the left (B), return to centre (SP) and so on. Rest and repeat. Tempo: medium.

SP. A SP B SP x 4

SP

A

B Keeping your weight equal on both feet, move your pelvis to the left, without shifting your upper body.

B

SP

Sequence 2 In a similar pattern to Sequence 1, you will tilt your pelvis forward and back. Thus, from SP, tilt forward (C), return to centre (SP), tilt back (D), return to centre (SP), and so on until you complete eight sets of two counts. Repeat.

SP. C SP D SP x 4

C

C Tuck your pelvis under, tilting it up and forward without leaning into the thighs. Keep the movement small and precise.

D

D Tilt the pelvis back and out. As you move your buttocks out, there will be a tendency to arch too much in the spine, thereby swaying the back and sticking the ribs out. Try to resist this.

Leg Flicks

One of the characteristics of jazz dance is a rhythmic play between the movement and the beat. You will frequently be moving very fast and then holding very still. These leg flicks are good exercises for developing the speed and agility you will need to make the stillness register. Practise them slowly at first, and then gradually increase the speed. Be careful with the tempo when flicking your leg out to the side as this involves fitting in an extra position.

The Sequence The pattern consists of three leg flicks, which you can do in six sets of four counts (two sets for each flick) or you can use this popular dance count: and-a-one (pause), and-a-two (pause), etc. The *and* corresponds to the first count, the *a* to the second, the *one* or *two* to the third, and the *pause* to the fourth. Starting at SP, bring your right leg up (A), flick it out in front of you (B), bend it back in (A), and return to SP. Then bring your right leg up again (A), turn it out to the side (C), flick it sharply out (D), return to passé (C), turn parallel (A), and return to SP. Lift your right leg up again (A), flick it back (E), bend it behind (F), bring it up in front (A), and return to SP. Repeat, then do the sequence twice on the other side. Tempo: fast.

SP. A B A SP A C D C A SP A E F A SP
x 4 (2 each side)

SP Start in a parallel plié position, arms open to 2nd. Hold your back very strongly so that you can isolate the legs and hold your balance straight through the centre.

D Flick your right leg sharply up and out to a high 2nd position. Try not to lift the right hip or lean the torso to the left.

C Turn your right leg out in the hip socket, keeping the toes touching the inside of your left leg.

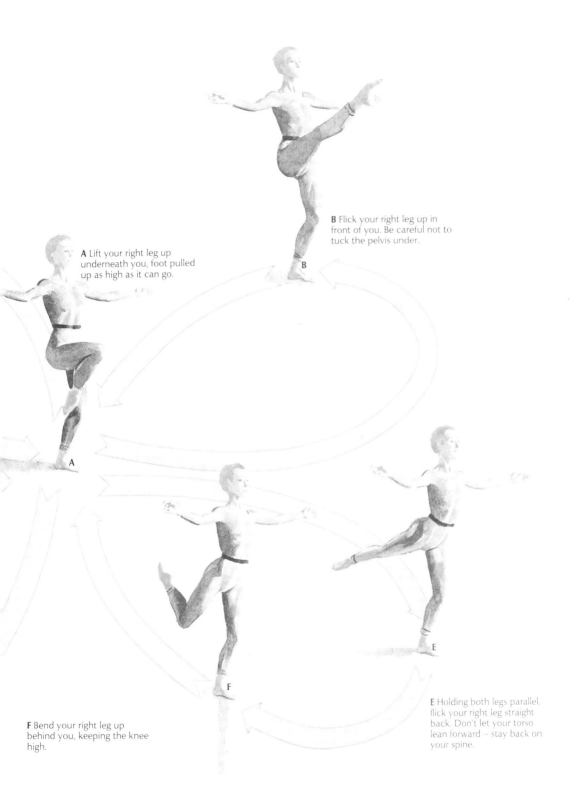

B Flick your right leg up in front of you. Be careful not to tuck the pelvis under.

A Lift your right leg up underneath you, foot pulled up as high as it can go.

E Holding both legs parallel, flick your right leg straight back. Don't let your torso lean forward – stay back on your spine.

F Bend your right leg up behind you, keeping the knee high.

Jazz Walks

Jazz walks are a fun way of getting into the feeling of jazz dance. The most important thing to remember is that the hip movement must come from the way you move your legs, not your pelvis. Imagine you are waiting for a bus. Stand with your legs together, then let your weight sag into one hip and relax down. The leg that takes the weight will be straight, the relaxing leg bent forward at the knee. Now put on some music with a Latin beat and try shifting your weight from leg to leg in time to the music. You will notice that the relaxing leg makes a small involuntary movement as you shift your weight. If you move this leg forward each time it happens you will find yourself doing the jazz walk.

Sequence 1 To jazz walk sideways to the right, starting at SP, shift your weight to your left hip and move your right leg across (A), then shift your weight on to your right hip and move your left leg across (B). Continue moving sideways for eight counts, shifting your weight on each count. Then take eight counts to move back to SP. As you change from right to left, your hips will stay the same on the eighth and first count. Tempo: medium.

SP. A B x 4 (right). **A B** x 3. **A** (left) **SP**

SP Stand in parallel 1st position, arms by your sides.

A Shift your weight to your left hip, keeping your left leg very straight, and bend your right leg as you move it out to your right side. Your whole back will compensate by curving over to your left. Drop your left shoulder and slightly lift your right. At the same time, bend your left elbow and pull it back and in.

B Complete the sideways step by shifting your weight on to your right leg, straightening your right knee, bending your left leg and bringing it in close to your right. Drop your right shoulder and bend your right arm at the elbow.

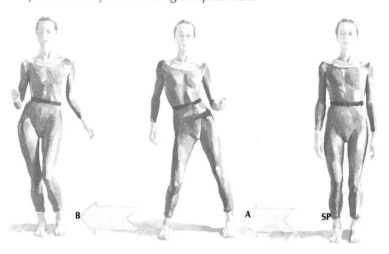

Sequence 2 To jazz walk forward, hold your head and torso slightly back, moving your legs as if you were being pushed up from underneath. Starting at SP, walk forward (C, D, C, D etc.) for eight counts and then backward for another eight, keeping your steps small. Going back your front leg will straighten as it pushes your weight up and back.

SP. C D x 4 (forward). **C D** x 3. **C** (backward) **SP**

C Shift your weight to your left hip, as in A, keeping your left leg straight, but move your right leg forward. Bend your left elbow and pull it in.

D Straighten your right leg and shift your weight on to it. Bend your left leg and move it forward.

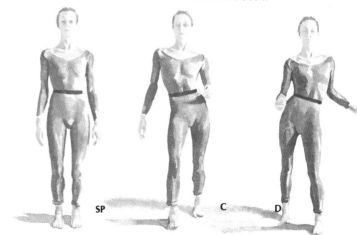

Back Side Forward Kick

A good way to develop a strong use of the legs in movement is the Back Side Forward Kick. You will be able to throw your whole weight into the kick – as a matter of fact, you will be able to use so much force that, once you have learned the pattern, you should be careful not to overstretch the long tendon running down the back of the leg. Keep your torso up and straight throughout the exercise, and your arms out to the sides.

The Sequence Do the exercise in four counts. Starting at SP, step back (A) 1, step back and to the side (B) 2, lunge forward (C) 3, and kick up (D) 4. Repeat on the other side, swinging your left leg from D back to position A on the left side, passing momentarily through SP but not stopping there. Alternate sides for eight counts of four. Tempo: medium.

SP. A B C D x 8 (4 each side). **SP**

SP Stand in parallel 1st position, feet close together and knees bent in a small demi-plié. Using your back muscles, hold your arms out to the sides very strongly so that they hold their position as you do the exercise.

A Step back on the right leg, holding the demi-plié.

B Bring the left foot back, passing diagonally across to your right ankle and then out to the left side.

C Shift your weight over to your left side and pass your right foot close by your left ankle. Lunge forward on to your right leg, allowing your left heel to rise off the floor.

D Shift your weight on to the right leg and swing your left leg straight through and up in front of you. Keep the standing leg in demi-plié.

SP   A   B   C   D

Parallel Jumps

As you have probably learned by now, an accurate parallel position is just as difficult to hold as a good turn out. These parallel jumps with quarter-turns are a logical follow-on from Jump Preparations (p.87), only they are done in a parallel position, rather than turned out. Although each jump is made independently of the others, there should be a feeling of bounce to the movement, making the jumps easier to do. Make sure that you turn your entire torso on the quarter-turn, not just your eyes or your legs. Try to be very precise about the way you place your feet on landing – a mirror can be a useful aid to checking your body placement.

A Spring straight up into the air, carefully holding your legs parallel and stretching them strongly down through the toes. Go straight up into the air – be careful not to heave your chest back.

The Sequence You will actually be doing a quarter-turn at the top of every other jump, so that in eight jumps you will have done a complete 360-degree turn. Starting at SP, spring up into the air (A), land facing front (SP), spring up again and do a quarter-turn (A), land facing right (B), spring up (C), land (B), spring up and turn right (C), land facing behind (D), and so on until you have completed eight jumps and are facing front (SP) again. Then do eight jumps to the left, all without stopping. Take four sets of two counts for each complete turn, landing on the beat. Tempo: medium.

SP. A SP A B C B C D (A) D (A B C B C) SP x 2 (both sides)

Note: Positions in parentheses indicate that the correct position is the mirror image of the one shown.

SP Start in a strong parallel position, arms down at the sides and held strongly in place so that they don't move around on the turns. As you plié to take the first jump, check that your knees go straight forward over your middle toes.

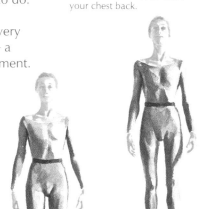

SP   A

B Land facing right in plié. If you are working in front of a mirror, check in this position that you have kept your body placement – spine long and straight and feet parallel.

C Spring straight up into the air again, pointing your toes and keeping your head lifted.

D Land facing behind in plié. Keep the same checks on your body position. Make sure your arms turn with you, and are not left slightly behind.

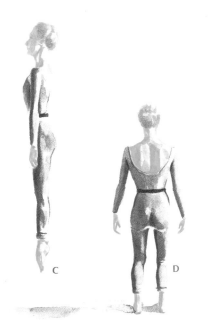

B   C   D

Bent Knee Jumps

Once you have learnt to jump straight up clearly and with control, the next stage is to jump and change your shape in mid-air. It will help if you have a very clear mental picture of the shape you must make in the air before actually attempting it – study the illustrations below and think of your muscles and the actions they must make. Sense the speed of the action, the fleeting pause for the position, and the action to return to the floor. Try the jumps one at a time at first before doing them in sequence. Remember that to jump well you must coordinate your legs and arms exactly, otherwise you will lose your balance.

Sequence 1 The starting and landing positions (1st position parallel plié, arms by your sides – referred to here as SP) are not illustrated, but by now you should know the position from memory. The exercise is in two counts. Starting in SP, spring into the air (A), land (SP) on count one, spring into the air again (B), and land (SP) on count two. Do eight alternate jumps, then rest and repeat again. Tempo: medium.

SP. A SP B SP x 4

A Spring into the air, pulling your legs up under you. Lift your knees up slightly in front of you, so that you seem to be sitting on your legs in the air. Open your arms out to 2nd.

B Spring into the air, turning out sharply as you leave the ground. Throw your thighs open, pull your knees up and bring your heels up to your buttocks. Again, you should appear to be sitting in the air, holding your arms out to the sides. Turn back to parallel before landing.

Sequence 2 The jumps in C and D are parallel attitude jumps. Starting in the basic parallel plié position (SP), spring into the air (C), land (SP), jump up again (D) and land in SP. Do eight jumps in eight single counts, landing on the beat each time. Rest and repeat.

SP. C SP D SP x 4

C Jump into the air, bringing the right thigh up in front of you and the left leg up behind you. Both knees should be bent so that the lower legs are at right angles to the thighs. Stretch both feet and throw your arms from the back into basic opposition, left arm forward, right arm out to the side.

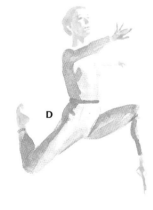

D This jump is the same as jump C, but on the other side. Your left leg should be forward and your right leg back, your right arm forward and your left arm to the side.

Jazz Walks with Arms

This jazz walk is similar to the Low Walk (p.93) but far more complex in terms of coordination, since it involves moving each arm independently with every step forward. Learn to do the walk first, then practise the arm movements one at a time, before adding them to the walk. One arm goes up, out to 2nd position, then straight down while the other arm simply goes up and down. Both arms bend in to the chest on the starting and intermediate positions. Once you can coordinate the arms, practise them with the body tilt and finally add both arms and body tilt to the walk. This will teach you clearly the kind of double thinking that is necessary for smooth arm and leg coordination.

SP Start with your weight forward on your left leg, both legs turned out, your right leg bent behind you on the half-toe. Bend both arms in toward your chest, palms flat, fingers almost touching.

A Lift both arms up overhead as you stretch and point your right leg forward. Tilt your body in the direction of your extending leg.

B Take your weight on to your right leg and bring both arms in to your chest, elbows out. Tilt your body to the left as you prepare to bring your left leg through.

C Lower your left arm down and extend your right arm out to 2nd as you stretch and point your left leg forward.

D Take your weight on to your left leg and bring both arms in to your chest, elbows out. Tilt your body to the right.

E Raise your left arm up overhead and lower your right arm down by your side. Stretch and point your right leg forward.

The Sequence As this sequence is very difficult, practise the walk first, then the arm movements. and when you have perfected both, try putting them together. The walk consists of six steps forward taken in six counts (and then the sequence is repeated). The count is taken with your weight held on the back leg (as in A, C, E, G, I, K); the "and" beats are taken as your weight transfers to the front leg. Stretch the leg long and luxuriously out to hit the beat each time, tilting your torso as you take your weight on to the front leg on the "and".

Now practise the arms, singly at first, then both together. The right arm will go up (A), then out to 2nd (C), straight down (E), and then start up again (G, I, K). The left arm will simply go up and down. Between each arm position, you will bring both arms in to your chest (on the "and" beat). After every sixth count, both arms will go up overhead, to repeat the pattern. When you can do the arm movements, add them to the jazz walk, tilting your body as you bring your arms in to your chest. Do the walk for 12 counts, and then change sides, leading off on your left leg and doing three arm positions (up, side, down) with your left arm. Tempo: medium.

SP. A B C D E F G H I J K SP x 4 (2 each side)

H Bring both arms in to your chest as you take your weight on to your left leg (as in D).

I Lift your left arm up overhead and extend your right arm out to 2nd. Stretch and point your right leg forward.

J Take your weight on to your right leg, tilt your body to the left and bring both arms in to your chest (as in B, F).

K Lower both arms down by your sides as you stretch your left leg forward.

F Bring both arms in to your chest as you take your weight on to your right leg (as in B).

G Lower your left arm down and raise your right arm up overhead as you stretch your left leg forward.

Travelling Jump with Contraction

Like many jazz movements, this travelling step, based on the skip (p.96) uses fast changes of body angle and quick jumps to put the emphasis on the movement itself. As you take the two running steps, throw your back strongly into opposition so that you have the strength of your back to help you sustain the jump. The contraction in the jump should help you to go up into the air, not throw you down. Think of the curve of the torso going diagonally across the body from your left hip to your right shoulder. With the assistance of the contraction and the lift of the legs, you should be able to go higher in this jump than you normally can.

The Sequence You should be able to run and jump in two counts. On the first count, run on to your left leg (A); on the second, run on to your right leg (B), jump (C, D) and land (E). Repeat the pattern five times, moving off on A (from E). Do six jumps on the other side. Tempo: fast.

SP. A B C D E x 12 (6 each side)

SP Start with your right leg forward and turned out, and your left leg bent back. Hold your arms in open opposition, left arm forward, right arm out to the side.

A Run forward on to your left leg, swinging your body and your right arm to the left, but still keeping the turn out.

B Run on to your right leg, swinging your body to the right. Hold both arms out to the sides.

C With your weight on your right leg, lift your left leg to the front, turned in.

D Push off into the air from your right leg. As you go up, contract your torso, curving your back and tucking your right leg up underneath you, parallel to your left leg. Hold both arms strongly out to the side – they will help you go up and stay in the air.

E Open your right leg out to land, releasing your torso at the same time. Cushion your weight through your right leg, keeping your torso high. Your left leg should be ready to move forward and take your weight again, as in A.

Jazz Workout Chart

The jazz exercises in this book are not sufficient to make a full class in themselves, so I have combined them with some floor exercises which will warm you up in readiness for the jazz dance. You will see that I have also included the jump exercises from Basic Centrework (pp.87-8) to prepare you for the parallel, bent-knee and travelling jumps. If you decide to learn these jazz dance movements, it is best to concentrate on them alone for a few weeks. Once you have mastered them, include one or two sessions a week in your workout.

FLOORWORK

Sitting spine stretches	
Breathing	
Contractions	
Contractions	D
Leg exercises	
Leg exercises	
Arm exercises	B
Side stretches	
Heel in hand stretches	D
Parallel leg flexes	
Combination flex and point	D
Hip spiral	D
Side falls	D
Leg lifts and spine stretches	D
Contractions arches	D
Kneeling spine curls	B
Kneeling spine curls	D
Rising from the floor	B
Rising from the floor	D

JAZZ		
	Body rolls	●
	Tendues with pliés	●
	Flex and point	●
	Jazz 4th	●
	Jazz 4th contraction	●
	Head rolls	●
	Shoulder isolations	●
	Shoulder isolations with contraction	●
	Rib isolations	●
	Hip isolations	●
	Leg flicks	●
	Jazz walks	●
	Back side forward kick	●
Basic Centrework	Jump preparations and jumps	●
	Parallel jumps	●
	Bent knee jumps	●
	Jazz walk with arms	●
	Travelling jumps	●

Taking Care of Yourself

A healthy body is not just a body that is free from illness —
it is a body that exudes well-being both physically and
mentally. So many people take their bodies for granted that
they abuse them without thought, spending long hours
sitting uncomfortably, snatching meals and taking little or no
exercise. Indeed, some people tend to take far better care of
the replaceable objects around them than they do of their
own bodies.

Since your body is your dancing instrument, it is up to you
to take care of it. Acquiring a fit and healthy body is not just
a matter of taking regular exercise, but of eating sensibly, not
smoking or drinking to excess, relaxing properly and getting
enough sleep. Below I have outlined some of the ways you
should be taking care of yourself. Take heed — for you are the
one who will ultimately benefit.

Warming Up
As with any form of exercise, it is
essential that you warm up before
working out. Do whatever makes
you feel more prepared to work —
some gentle stretching exercises,
for instance, to loosen up your
muscles and increase your pulse
rate. Take note of the temperature
in the room. The colder it is, the
longer you will need to warm up.
Don't warm up by kicking your
legs up in the air — your body will
not be ready for this sudden exer-
tion. Most injuries happen outside
of class when people are not working progressively but erratically.

Cooling Down
Cooling down at the end of a workout is very important if you've
been working hard. All the time
you've been exercising, an
increased amount of blood has
been pumped around your body. If
you stop abruptly, the blood will
tend to "pool" in your extremities,
causing you to feel dizzy. If you
slow down gradually, however, by
doing some passive stretching
exercises, your muscles will
continue to assist your blood flow
and your pulse rate will return to
normal. Massaging aching muscles
can also relieve post-exercise stiff-
ness. Make sure you put on some
warm clothes so that your body
doesn't cool too rapidly.

Massaging aching feet

Treating Injuries
An injury (provided it is not
inflicted by someone else) is
nature's way of saying "slow
down". All dancers suffer injury at
some time in their lives. If it is a
straightforward swelling from a fall,
the best thing to do is to put ice
on it, taking care not to give yourself frostbite. After the first day of
ice treatment, try alternate hot
and cold compresses (10 minutes
each) for about 40 minutes. Repeat
every four hours.

If you hear a loud snap or feel
that you were kicked or struck by
someone, go to an emergency
clinic *at once*. In fact, even with
the smallest injury, if in any doubt,
always seek medical advice.

Learning to Relax

Relaxation is as essential as movement – when one set of muscles contracts, another set relaxes. Most of us feel we know how to relax – but how many know how to do it properly? More often than not, when we think we are relaxed, we are gripping the arm of a chair, or we are sitting in a hunched-up position.

If you have time, try to relax for a short period after each workout. A good method of relaxation is the corpse pose, a classic yoga position. Lie on your back, feet apart, and hands away from your sides, palms up. Feel that your body is symmetrical, letting your thighs, legs and toes turn out. Close your eyes and breathe deeply, allowing gravity to embrace you. Rotate your legs in and out, and then your arms. Breathe deeply and slowly, and empty all thoughts from your mind.

The Corpse Pose

A Healthy Diet

If you have a weight problem, dance training will help you to get back into better shape, but it won't help you to lose it. Not unless you work hard for several hours a day and sweat copiously. The only way to rid yourself of those unwanted pounds is to exercise *and* diet – and by dieting, I do not mean crash dieting. You must completely change your outlook on food, and this applies to everyone, whether they have a weight problem or not.

If you want to look and feel better, there are five simple rules:

1. Cut down on animal fats and all saturated fats.
2. Avoid refined and processed foods – foods that are low in fibre and high in chemical additives.
3. Reduce your intake of sugar.
4. Cut down on salty foods.
5. Emphasize whole grains, fresh fruit and vegetables, nuts and yogurt.

Try to eat regularly and sensibly. When you eat can be quite an important factor in controlling your weight. Ideally you should eat breakfast and lunch, so that you will be less inclined to want a large meal in the evening. (Remember that your body needs time to metabolize the food before you go to sleep.) Never exercise on a full stomach – you will feel uncomfortable and your circulation will be confused by conflicting demands. Similarly, never exercise on an empty one – you will feel weak and unable to concentrate. If you do feel the need for sugar when working, eat fruit that is naturally sweet, such as dates or bananas.

There seems little doubt that the combination of a healthy diet and regular exercise is a winning one. It is up to you to follow it.

What Next?

If you have managed to complete the work in this book and are working through the exercises with some competence, you may be attracted to the idea of becoming a performance dancer. If so, there are several options open to you, but before I enlarge on them, I ought to warn you of some of the pitfalls ahead.

The working life of a performance dancer is short. True, dancers can perform well into their forties, but in most cases their ability to jump becomes drastically reduced, and they begin to lose speed and attack. Not only is the working life of a dancer short, but it is also extremely arduous. Dancers must and do take a daily class and rehearse for hours on end. At LCDT, the dancers took an hour-and-a-half class and then rehearsed for six hours every rehearsal day. On a performance day, they took a one-hour class and rehearsed for three hours *as well as* the performance.

You will also have to be free to travel constantly, which may put a strain on personal relationships. At times you may find that you are only at home a few months in the year.

In short, you will have to be highly motivated, self-disciplined and, to a certain extent, self-sufficient. If all this doesn't put you off, read on!

A dancing career can be very rewarding. It deeply satisfies an urge in all of us to be individual and to be in some part in control of our lives. When a performance goes well, the experience of being part of that performance and to have brought pleasure to so many people, is reward enough for all those weeks of hard work.

To become a dancer you must have a good body – and look after it well. As you should have learnt from the exercises, you will have to become more flexible, open

joints and reshape muscles – all of which demand a body that is still capable of physical change, not one that has become fixed through age or mental attitude. I started training when I was 21 – for me, it was not too late. But as a general rule, the earlier in life you start, the better.

With regard to training, I cannot stress how important it is for you to obtain the best there is. Any kind of good training is better than bad or indifferent training. So many students are turned away at auditions simply because they have been poorly trained. What kind of training you should apply for depends very much on the kind of dance you are interested in. It is possible now to have a good technical training and work for a degree at the same time at a full-time dance academy. You can train as a theatre dancer, performance dancer, teacher or even as a choreographer.

If you can't attend a full-time dance school, then it is up to you to take at least two technique classes a day. As soon as you are satisfied with your performance, apply for auditions. Remember – still keep up your daily training! There are many small experimental groups with a fairly regular turnover in dancers so, if you like what they do, ask to be put on their list for an audition. Weekly theatrical papers list auditions, and you will find notices on bulletin boards in most large dance centres.

Good dancers are a special breed of people. They require a strange combination of intuition and logic, of passion and control. They have to be able to overcome disappointment and succeed. But, as all good dancers know, when they do succeed, the rewards are immeasurable. Very few people attain true excellence.

Above: Michael Small and Lauren Potter in *Eos* (1978). Choreographer Robert Cohan.

Below: The Company in *Second Turning* (1982). Choreographer Christopher Bannerman.

Glossary

Adagio   A controlled sequence of movement done very slowly and smoothly.

Arabesque   A position in which you balance on one leg and extend the other leg behind. Both legs should be turned out.

Attitude   A turned out position in which you balance on one leg and lift the other leg forward or back with the knee bent at about 90° to the thigh.

Deep plié   A full bend of the knees, where your heels naturally come up off the floor.

Demi-plié   Literally a "half-bend". The knees are bent keeping the heels on the floor. Remember to keep your knees in line with your toes.

Isolation   With particular reference to jazz, an isolation is the independent movement of any single muscle group or joint.

Opposition   A natural process of spiralling which occurs as you walk. When the right leg comes forward, the left arm will come forward in opposition, and vice versa.

Parallel   A position in which the thighs, knees and toes of both legs are facing straight ahead. Just as you have 1st and 2nd positions in turn out, so you can have the same positions in parallel. In contemporary dance they are normally referred to as parallel closed (1st) and parallel wide (2nd).

Passé   Standing on one leg, bend your other knee up and touch the inside knee of your standing leg with pointed toes in a passing through movement.

Plié   A bend of the knees.

Relevé   Lifted or raised up on the half-toe.

Sickled foot   A term used to describe the foot when it is twisted in a curve toward the big toe.

Tendu   Stretched.

Turned out   A position in which the thighs, knees and toes are turned out and away from each other. There are five turned out positions for the feet: *1st*, in which your heels should be placed together; *2nd*, in which you stand with your feet apart (separated by about one-and-a-half times the length of your foot); *3rd*, in which the heel of one foot is placed against the instep of the other, marking the beginning of the body spiralling into space; *4th*, in which one foot is placed in front of the other (the feet being separated by the distance you can stretch and point the front foot); and *5th* in which the body spiral is pulled tight by placing one foot directly in front of the other, heel to toe.

Index

Index of Dancers

Picture Credits
All photographs in this book were taken by Fausto Dorelli, with the following exceptions: *p.17* Japanese or Manchurian cranes by Orion Press/Tsutomu Tsutsui, courtesy of Bruce Coleman Ltd; *p.19* Balinese dancers by Sandro Pato, courtesy of Bruce Coleman Ltd; *p.189* LCDT dancers by Robert Cohan.

Author's Acknowledgements
First of all I must thank Joss Pearson of Gaia Books for coming to us with the idea. We had long thought of doing a book on technique but without her encouragement it would not have happened. Many thanks also to Lucy Lidell who helped to formulate the ideas and plan the book; Michele Staple who made the text readable and corrected all the spelling; Sara Mathews and Chris Meehan who, in the course of designing the book, had to learn to dance as well; Kerry Woodward and Julian Moss who posed for the artwork; Linda Gibbs who also posed for artwork and assisted with the project; Jane Darling who assisted with the jazz section and helped me to remember my work with Jack Cole some 25 years ago; Barbara Karban for the use of her imaginative illustrations; Antony van Laast, Patrick Harding-Irmer and Anca Frankenhaeuser who read through and checked the exercises; Janet Eager and Jane Ward at London Contemporary Dance Theatre who organized models

for the photographic sessions and dealt with the endless meetings; the dancers of LCDT and the students who interrupted their busy schedule to pose; and Fausto Dorelli for his beautiful photographs.

Most of all, thanks go to Martha Graham who taught me how to dance, and to all of my students over the years who taught me how to teach.

Publisher's Acknowledgements
Gaia would like to extend special thanks to: Keith Allison; Michael Burman; Granville Dolan of Hourds Typographica; Fausto Dorelli and Peter; Linda Gibbs; Lesley Gilbert; Barbara Karban; Lucy Lidell; Peter Mennim; Sheilagh Noble; Joe Robinson; Ann Savage; Wayne Sleep; Antony van Laast; Sally Welford.